Financial Accounting is NOT That Hard!

Understand Financial Information

Janice L. Cobb, CPA

530 Great Road
Acton, Massachusetts 01720
800-562-2147

Table of Contents

Financial Accounting is NOT That Hard!
Understand Financial Information

Chapter:		Begins on Page:
1.	Overview of Financial Statements	1
2.	The Balance Sheet	13
3.	Things that Change the Balance Sheet	31
4.	The Income Statement	39
5.	More on the Income Statement	49
6.	Revenues and Expenses Change the Balance Sheet	65
7.	The Statement of Stockholders' Equity	83
8.	The Cash Flow Statement	87
9.	Footnotes and Other Information	99
10.	Financial Statement Analysis	109
11.	Accounting Estimates and Other Things to Consider	127

Appendix A: Gathering Data and Preparing the Financial Statements

A-1	Recording Business Transactions	147
A-2	Record Journal Entries and Balance Accounts	155
A-3	Adjustments to Accounts	167
A-4	Finishing the Accounting and Reporting Process	177

Preface and Introduction

Janice Cobb has taught Financial Accounting to undergraduates, MBAs, and executives of major corporations at Texas Christian University for the past fifteen years. She grew tired of seeing the looks of frustration on her students' faces, listened as they told her the things they did not understand, and developed a method of learning financial accounting that is extremely easy to understand. You will understand financial accounting after reading this book.

This book will teach you about the language of accounting and finance and how accountants determine reported values. You will be able to read and understand the four financial statements like a professional. Accounting is not math. Accountants add, subtract, multiply and divide using a calculator. Accounting is how companies explain their financial position and the results of operating the business to those outside the company.

All businesses participate in similar types of activities in hopes of receiving more from customers than the cost to provide to customers. It requires all four financial statements and footnotes to report the results of business operations from different perspectives. This book teaches you how the following typical business activities are reported on the four financial statements:

1) Obtain money from investors and lenders.
2) Buy items used to operate the business.
3) Provide goods and services to customers.
4) Receive services from others in order to operate the business.
5) Use items to operate the business.

Most other accounting books teach you how to read financial statements by explaining the format of the statements, providing definitions of account names and demonstrating how accountants record a few simple transactions for each statement. It is very difficult for most people to understand how to record transactions and prepare financial statements without a solid understanding of the language. As such, there is a general <u>perception</u> that accounting is hard to understand. <u>Accounting is not hard</u> to understand when the language is familiar and the concepts are related to simple every day business operations.

This book makes it easy to understand accounting by using a step by step approach to explain the following:

1) The language of business.
2) The purpose of each financial statement.
3) How the most common types of business transactions are reported on the financial statements.
4) How common business transactions change each financial statement.
5) Estimates and other issues that affect reported financial information.
6) Financial statement analysis used to make investment decisions.

Preface and Introduction (continued)

If you are currently enrolled in an accounting class and would like practice problems and additional information, please visit www.studymyaccounting.com. Select the maroon tab, *Introduction to Accounting*. The study materials on this website provide outlines and practice tests with fully explained answers in an easy to understand step by step manner. The website provides detail information on accounts receivables, inventory, property and equipment, intangible assets, liabilities, equity transactions, earnings per share, preparing the cash flow statement, managerial accounting, and a variety of other topics beyond the scope of this book.

1. Overview of Financial Statements

Accounting is the language of business. Anyone who has (or wants to have) excess money must know how to speak the language and read financial information in order to make good financial decisions.

Accounting is the process of identifying and communicating financial information to investors, lenders and other decision makers. Financial information is any data that can be measured and reported in dollars. There are many different ways to present and value financial information. Accountants follow standard methods of reporting financial information to make it easier for all to understand. Insight into the methods used by accountants is necessary to understand financial information.

Financial accounting is not just used by accountants; it is used by all business people. Business people must be able to tell others outside the company about the financial position and earnings of the company. They must also understand the factors that change the financial position and profitability of the company. A solid understanding of financial information is necessary to be a successful business person.

Lenders (creditors) loan money in order to earn more money. Investors provide funds to others in order to participate in the growth of a company and earn a return on their investment. A decision to loan or invest money should not be made without reviewing and understanding reliable financial information.

Accounting and finance professionals rely on four financial statements to help them determine the financial position and performance of an organization. Each financial statement presents financial information from a different perspective.

The four financial statements are as follows:

> 1) Balance Sheet (also called Statement of Financial Position.)
>
> 2) Income Statement (also called Statement of Operations.)
>
> 3) Statement of Stockholders' Equity (also called Statement of Shareholders' Equity.)
>
> 4) Statement of Cash Flows (also called Cash Flow Statement)

Amounts presented on the financial statements may be reported at cost, adjusted cost, fair market value, present value of future cash flows, or a variety of other economic measurements. Words presented on financial statements may have more than one meaning. Financial reports are prepared according to generally accepted accounting principles to ensure items with the same meaning are called essentially the same name and amounts are valued fairly consistent from company to company.

The Purpose of Each Financial Statement

Each financial statement provides different information about the business. Together, all four financial statements give a fairly complete summary of a company's financial position and results of operations.

The balance sheet reports three types of items:

1) What the company **has and uses to operate the business; called assets.**

2) What the company **owes; called liabilities.**

3) The amount of the company **owned by the owners; called stockholders' equity.**
   (Assets less liabilities equal stockholders' equity.)

All amounts reported on the balance sheet are **cumulative** as of the specified date of the statement. Amounts represent the net result of everything that has happened since the company's first day of business up to and including the specified date.

The balance sheet reports how a company financed its operations (from owners or borrowings), items a company uses to operate the business (cash, inventory, equipment, etc.), and the portion of the assets that are owned.

A personal balance sheet as of December 31st would look like the following:

Assets:		Liabilities:	
Cash	300	Monthly bills not yet paid	220
Insurance paid for six months	450	(utilities, cable, phone)	
Office supplies	60	Credit card balance owed	1,860
Food	85		
Receivable from brother	200	Owed for auto	13,290
		Owed to parents	2,600
Automobile	15,200	Owed on mortgage	80,000
Computer equipment	2,400	Total Liabilities	97,970
Furniture & fixtures	1,850		
House	100,000	Stockholders' Equity:	
		Retained earnings	22,575
		Total Stockholders' Equity	22,575
Total Assets	120,545	Total Liabilities and Stockholders' Equity	120,545

The personal balance sheet reports things owned and used, amounts owed to others, and earnings used to purchase items owned. The personal balance sheet seems fairly straight forward and easy to understand because the words are familiar. The balance sheet for Walt Disney Company below also reports what is owned and used in the business, amounts owed to others, and amounts contributed by owners.

Walt Disney Company
CONSOLIDATED BALANCE SHEETS
(in millions, except per share data)

	October 2, 2010	October 1, 2011
ASSETS		
Cash and cash equivalents	$2,722	$3,185
Receivables	5,784	6,182
Inventories	1,442	1,595
Television costs	678	674
Deferred income taxes	1,018	1,487
Other current assets	581	634
Total current assets	12,225	13,757
Film and television costs	4,773	4,357
Investments	2,513	2,435
Parks, resorts and other property, at cost Attractions, buildings and equipment	32,875	35,515
Accumulated depreciation	(18,373)	(19,572)
	14,502	15,943
Projects in progress	2,180	2,625
Land	1,124	1,127
	17,806	19,695
Intangible assets, net	5,081	5,121
Goodwill	24,100	24,145
Other assets	2,708	2,614
	$69,206	$72,124
LIABILITIES AND EQUITY		
Accounts payable and other accrued liabilities	$6,109	$6,362
Current portion of borrowings	2,350	3,055
Unearned royalties and other advances	2,541	2,671
Total current liabilities	11,000	12,088
Borrowings	10,130	10,922
Deferred income taxes	2,630	2,866
Other long-term liabilities	6,104	6,795
Commitments and contingencies (Note 15)		

Walt Disney Company Balance Sheet continued:

Equity		
Preferred stock, $.01 par value		
Authorized — 100 million shares, Issued — none	—	—
Common stock, $.01 par value		
Authorized — 4.6 billion shares; Issued — 2.7 billion shares	28,736	30,296
Retained earnings	34,327	38,375
Accumulated other comprehensive loss	(1,881)	(2,630)
	61,182	66,041
Treasury stock, at cost, 803.1 million shares at October 2, 2010 and 937.8 million shares at October 1, 2011	(23,663)	(28,656)
Total Disney Shareholder's equity	37,519	37,385
Noncontrolling interests	1,823	2,068
Total Equity	39,342	39,453
Total liabilities and equity	$69,206	$72,124

Walt Disney Company's balance sheet is much more difficult to read because many of the words are not familiar. The meaning of the account names and amounts are explained in detail in chapter 2 and chapter 6.

The income statement reports the following items:

1) The value of goods or services provided to customers during a period of time.

2) The cost of providing goods or services to customers during a period of time.

3) Net earnings for a period of time.

Net earnings is the value of goods and services provided to customers
less the cost of providing to customers during a specific period of time.
The specific period of time is typically a month, a quarter, or a year.

A personal income statement for the month of December would look like the following:

Service Revenue (paycheck)	1,200
Insurance Expense	(55)
Rent Expense	(525)
Food Expense	(210)
Utilities Expense	(90)
Cable and Internet Expense	(70)
Phone Expense	(75)
Interest Expense	(20)
Gasoline Expense	(130)
Net Income (Earnings)	25

The personal income statement reports amounts earned from providing services to others (revenues) and the cost of living to support the ability to work and provide to others. The income statement for Walt Disney Company presented below also reports services provided to others and the cost of providing to others.

Walt Disney Company
CONSOLIDATED STATEMENTS OF INCOME
(in millions, except per share data)

	2011	2010	2009
Revenues	$ 40,893	$ 38,063	$ 36,149
Costs and expenses	(33,112)	(31,337)	(30,452
Restructuring and impairment charges	(55)	(270)	(492)
Other income (expense)	75	140	342
Net interest expense	(343)	(409)	(466)
Equity in the income of investees	585	440	577
Income before income taxes	8,043	6,627	5,658
Income taxes	(2,785)	(2,314)	(2,049)
Net Income	5,258	4,313	3,609

The income statement for Walt Disney Company is more challenging to read and understand than the personal income statement. This is due to a lack of familiarity with the words and categories used on the income statement. The meaning of the line items, categories and amounts are explained in detail in chapter 5.

The statement of stockholders' equity reports the following items:

1) Funds investors (owners) contribute to the company in exchange for ownership.

2) Amounts paid back to investors (dividends.)

3) Earnings of the company attributed to the investors (owners.)

The statement of stockholders' equity is **for a period of time**; generally a month, a quarter, or a year.

A personal statement of stockholders' equity for the month of December would look like the following:

	Retained Earnings
Beginning Balance (November's Ending Balance)	22,550
+ Net Income (Earnings) for December	25
Ending Balance (Reported on the December Balance Sheet)	22,575

The statement of stockholders' equity reports all exchanges that occur directly with owners during the period. Owners are entitled to the earnings. All earnings kept in the company are referred to as retained earnings.

One year of the statement of shareholders' equity for Walt Disney Company is presented below. The statement for Walt Disney Company looks very complicated at first glance. Stockholders' equity items and exchanges with owners for a company are often much more complicated than from a personal perspective. The statement is set up the same way as the personal statement of stockholder's equity. A description of each exchange with owners is listed down the left side and the account names affected are listed across the top. Most of the words used by Walt Disney Company will be explained in chapter 2. The more complicated exchanges with owners are outside the scope of this book.

Walt Disney Company
CONSOLIDATED STATEMENTS OF SHAREHOLDERS' EQUITY
(in millions, except per share data)

| | Equity Attributable to Disney | | | | | | | |
	Shares	Common Stock	Retained Earnings	Accumulated Other Comprehensive Income (Loss)	Treasury Stock	Total Disney Equity	Non-controlling Interest	Total Equity
OCTOBER 3, 2009	1,861	$27,038	$31,033	$ (1,644)	$(22,693)	$33,734	$1,691	$35,425
Net income	—	—	3,963	—	—	3,963	350	4,313
Comprehensive income						3,726	338	4,064
Equity compensation activity	54	1,498	—	—	—	1,498	—	1,498
Acquisition of Marvel	59	188	—	—	1,699	1,887	90	1,977
Common stock repurchases	(80)	—	—	—	(2,669)	(2,669)	—	(2,669)
Dividends	—	9	(662)	—	—	(653)	—	(653)
Distributions and other	—	3	(7)	—	—	(4)	(296)	(300)
OCTOBER 2, 2010	1,894	$28,736	$34,327	$ (1,881)	$(23,663)	$37,519	$1,823	$39,342

The statement of cash flow reports information in three separate sections as follows:

The **operating activities** section reports the amount of cash generated from day to day operations and includes the following:

1) The amount of cash received from customers.

2) The amount of cash paid for services provided to the company.

3) The amount of cash paid for items used for day to day operations.

The **investing activities** section reports cash related to buying and selling assets used in the business for more than one year.

The **financing activities** section reports cash related to the following:

1) Borrowing and repaying debt.

2) Payments to and from owners.

The statement of cash flows is for a period of time, typically a month, a quarter, or a year.

A personal statement of cash flows for the month of December would look like the following (under the indirect method.)

Net Income	25
Change in Current Assets and Liabilities:	
Insurance for next month	(20)
Food in the kitchen	(49)
Net Cash used by Operating Activities	**(44)**
Purchase computer equipment	(600)
Purchase furniture	(400)
Sold computer equipment	215
Net Cash used in Investing Activities	**(785)**
Borrowings on credit card	110
Payment on auto loan	(199)
Net Cash from Financing Activities	**(89)**
Total Change in Cash	(918)
Beginning Cash Balance	1,218
Ending Cash Balance	**300**

The statement of cash flows for Walt Disney Company is presented below. This statement reports activities that change cash much the same way as the personal cash flow statement. This statement is difficult to read at this point because of the lack of familiarity with the meaning of the words. The cash flow statement is discussed further in chapter 8.

Walt Disney Company
CONSOLIDATED STATEMENTS OF CASH FLOWS
(in millions)

	2011	2010	2009
OPERATING ACTIVITIES			
Net income	$ 5,258	$ 4,313	$ 3,609
Depreciation and amortization	1,841	1,713	1,631
Gains on dispositions	(75)	(118)	(342)
Deferred income taxes	127	133	323
Equity in the income of investees	(585)	(440)	(577)
Cash distributions received from equity investees	608	473	505
Net change in film and television costs	332	238	(43)
Equity-based compensation	423	391	361
Impairment charges	16	132	279
Other	188	9	29
Changes in operating assets and liabilities			
Receivables	(518)	(686)	468
Inventories	(199)	(127)	(117)
Other assets	(189)	42	(565)
Accounts payable and other accrued liabilities	(367)	649	250
Income taxes	134	(144)	8
Cash provided by operations	**6,994**	**6,578**	**5,319**
INVESTING ACTIVITIES			
Investments in parks, resorts and other property	(3,559)	(2,110)	(1,753)
Proceeds from dispositions	564	170	185
Acquisitions	(184)	(2,493)	(176)
Other	(107)	(90)	(11)
Cash used in investing activities	**(3,286)**	**(4,523)**	**(1,755)**
FINANCING ACTIVITIES			
Commercial paper borrowings, net	393	(1,190)	(1,985)
Borrowings	2,350	--	1,750
Reduction of borrowings	(1,096)	(1,371)	(1,617)
Dividends	(756)	(653)	(648)
Repurchases of common stock	(4,993)	(2,669)	(138)
Exercise of stock options and other	857	840	(510)
Cash used in financing activities	**(3,245)**	**(2,750)**	**(3,148)**
(Decrease)/increase in cash and cash equivalents	463	(695)	416
Cash and cash equivalents, beginning of year	2,722	3,417	3,001
Cash and cash equivalents, end of year	**$ 3,185**	**$ 2,722**	**$ 3,417**

The four financial statements present a <u>summary</u> of financial information. Financial statements do not provide all the details needed to make good decisions. Additional details are stated in **footnotes** provided with the financial statements. Footnotes provide the following:

1) A description of the accounting methods followed.

2) Additional details related to items and amounts stated on the financial statements.

3) Additional information related to significant transactions of the company.

Accounting Guidance

The accounting profession has historically had an organization that issues guidance on how to provide the best and most useful financial information. The American Institute of Certified Public Accountants (AICPA) is the national association of practicing accountants. The AICPA was established in the early 1900s and is actively involved in establishing accounting guidance today. In 1939, the AICPA established the Committee on Accounting Procedures (CAP). The CAP, composed of practicing accountants, established 51 Accounting Research Bulletins (ARB) that provided accounting guidance on specific accounting issues. In 1959, the AICPA established the Accounting Principles Board (APB) to determine appropriate accounting practices. The APB, which consisted of about 20 practicing accountants, provided official accounting pronouncements called APB Opinions. In 1973, the Financial Accounting Foundation was established to select members of the **Financial Accounting Standards Board** (FASB). FASB is the organization that currently provides accounting guidance in the United States.

FASB's primary responsibility is to provide accounting guidance that improves the usefulness of financial information. FASB provides guidance for new business transactions and revises guidance previously issued as economic conditions and business transactions change. The majority of accounting guidance is related to the following:

1) The type of financial information that must be provided.

2) The format to use to provide information.

3) Measuring and valuing amounts reported on financial statements.

All accounting guidance is referred to collectively as **Generally Accepted Accounting Principles** (GAAP). GAAP means exactly as the name implies; generally accepted by accountants and financial service professionals that following the guidance will result in a reliable presentation of the economic results of operations and the financial position of a company. Accounting guidance is reviewed and accepted by accounting and finance professionals prior to issuance by the Financial Accounting Standards Board. Information related to current accounting issues is available on the FASB's website at www.FASB.org.

The **Securities Exchange Commission** (SEC) is the government entity that regulates the information public companies are required to provide to investors. The SEC requires public companies to follow GAAP and provide additional information to describe the operations of the business that is not presented in the financial statements or footnotes. Violation of SEC reporting requirements is a violation of law for public companies. There are currently approximately 6,000 companies that trade ownership shares on a public exchange in the United States. See chapter 9 for further discussion of SEC reporting requirements.

There is no law that requires GAAP to be followed by privately held companies. However, privately held companies that do not follow GAAP may find it very difficult to obtain money from outsiders. Investors and lenders with excess money generally do not have confidence in financial information that is not prepared in accordance with GAAP.

Public accounting firms provide the service of reviewing financial statements and footnotes before the financial information is provided to the general public. This service is called an **audit** and the public accounting firm is referred to as the **auditor**. The auditor provides an **auditor's report** that states whether or not the financial statements are fairly presented in accordance with GAAP. Fairly presented means a user of the financial information would not be misled when relying on the information to make a financial decision. Fairly presented does not mean the financial information is 100% accurate. It is common for financial statement of large companies to contain minor errors that are does not significantly change the interpretation of the financial information provided. All public companies are required to have an audit. Investors and creditors often require private companies to be audited in order to have a higher level of confidence in the information provided by the financial statements and footnotes. The auditor's report for AMR Corporation (the parent company of American Airlines) is presented at the end of this chapter.

The **Public Company Accounting Oversight Board** (PCAOB) was established by Congress in 2002 to establish standards that auditors must follow and review the methods used by auditors. These standards were established to bring consistency and credibility to the audit process.

Accounting principles and guidelines around the world differ. Many countries have their own financial accounting guidelines provided by an organization similar to FASB. Other countries follow accounting guidance provided by the **International Accounting Standards Board** (IASB), an organization that is attempting to standardize accounting guidance around the world. The IASB issues guidance under **International Financial Reporting Standards** (IFRS.)

Many companies currently operate internationally in many different parts of the world. Investing and lending is done from a worldwide perspective. Consistent accounting standards would make it easier to combine the accounting for all parts of international operations. There is a current movement to converge United States GAAP with IFRS. Progress toward standardized accounting guidance is being made; however, this is a slow process that could take years to fully accomplish. Discussion of various accounting requirements around the world is beyond the scope of this book.

Summary of Financial Information

Do not be concerned if you are feeling slightly overwhelmed at this point. The other chapters in the book will guide you through a solid understanding of financial information step by step. This chapter introduces the four financial statements. The key things that should be taken from this chapter are as follows:

The **balance sheet** reports the following:

1) Items the company has to use to operate the business (assets), amounts owed (liabilities), and amounts attributed to the owners (owners equity.)

2) Cumulative amounts as of a specific date. It does not report what happened to change amounts from one year to the next.

The **income statement** reports the following:

1) The value of services provided to customers (revenues)

2) The costs of providing to customers (expenses).

The income statement does not report cash because cash can be paid or received in a different period of time than the activity occurred.
This will be discussed in detail in chapters 4 and 5.

The **statement of stockholders' equity** reports the following:

1) Transactions directly with owners that may or may not be an exchange of cash.

The **cash flow statement** reports the following;

1) Amounts that are paid or received in cash from various activities.

Accountants typically provide financial statements to management inside the company each month. Private companies provide financial statements to their investors and creditors as requested. Public companies provide financial statements quarterly and at the end of each year. Public companies must follow the generally accepted accounting principles (GAAP) provided by the SEC and FASB. Financial statements for all public companies are available at www.sec.gov or on the company's website under investor information.

A very important part of being able to effectively use financial information is a strong understanding of the language used by accountants. You will learn the language in the next few chapters.

Report of Independent Registered Public Accounting Firm

The Board of Directors and Stockholders
AMR Corporation (Debtor and Debtor-in-Possession)

We have audited the accompanying consolidated balance sheets of AMR Corporation (Debtor and Debtor-in-Possession) (the Company) as of December 31, 2011 and 2010, and the related consolidated statements of operations, comprehensive income (loss), stockholders' equity (deficit) and cash flows for each of the three years in the period ended December 31, 2011. Our audits also included the financial statement schedule listed in the Index at Item 15(a)(2). These consolidated financial statements and schedule are the responsibility of the Company's management. Our responsibility is to express an opinion on these financial statements and schedule based on our audits.

We conducted our audits in accordance with the standards of the Public Company Accounting Oversight Board (United States). Those standards require that we plan and perform the audit to obtain reasonable assurance about whether the financial statements are free of material misstatement. An audit includes examining, on a test basis, evidence supporting the amounts and disclosures in the financial statements. An audit also includes assessing the accounting principles used and significant estimates made by management, as well as evaluating the overall financial statement presentation. We believe that our audits provide a reasonable basis for our opinion.

In our opinion, the financial statements referred to above present fairly, in all material respects, the consolidated financial position of AMR Corporation (Debtor and Debtor-in-Possession) at December 31, 2011 and 2010 and the consolidated results of its operations and its cash flows for each of the three years in the period ended December 31, 2011, in conformity with U.S. generally accepted accounting principles. Also, in our opinion, the related financial statement schedule, when considered in relation to the basic financial statements taken as a whole, presents fairly, in all material respects, the information set forth therein.

The accompanying consolidated financial statements have been prepared assuming that the Company will continue as a going concern. As discussed in Note 1 to the consolidated financial statements, the Company's bankruptcy filing raises substantial doubt about the Company's ability to continue as a going concern. Management's plans concerning these matters are described in Note 1. The consolidated financial statements do not include adjustments that might result from the outcome of this uncertainty.

We also have audited, in accordance with the standards of the Public Company Accounting Oversight Board (United States), the Company's internal control over financial reporting as of December 31, 2011, based on criteria established in Internal Control—Integrated Framework issued by the Committee of Sponsoring Organizations of the Treadway Commission and our report dated February 15, 2012 expressed an unqualified opinion thereon.

/s/ Ernst & Young LLP

Dallas, Texas
February 15, 2012

12

2. The Balance Sheet

The balance sheet reports the following two things:

    1) How funds (money) were raised to operate the business.

    2) Items the company has and uses to operate the business.

Money to operate the business come from the following two sources:

    1) **Investors:** Funds contributed by owners; does not have to be repaid.

    2) **Creditors:** Borrowed money; must be repaid.

The **owners** (investors) who originally establish the business **contribute money** to the company in exchange for shares of ownership. The original owners may also sell shares to others in order to obtain more cash. The total amount of cash received from all owners is reported on the balance sheet as **common stock and capital** under stockholders' equity.

Example 2-1: $75,000 is contributed to the company by the initial owners and $25,000 is received later by the company from additional owners. No distinction is made on the balance sheet between initial owners or other owners.

Assets:		Liabilities:	
Cash	$100,000		
		Stockholders' Equity:	
		Common Stock and capital	$100,000
Total Assets	$100,000	Total Liabilities & Stockholders' Equity	$100,000

Stock and capital represent funds received from investors in exchange for ownership.

The major advantage of obtaining funds from owners is the funds do not have to be repaid. The major disadvantage of issuing stock is that existing owners must share profits and decision making with the new owners.

Companies may also get money for operations or to purchase things necessary to run the company by **borrowing money** from various lenders (creditors.)

Money borrowed that must be repaid is called a **liability.** A liability must have **all** three of the following characteristics to be reported on the balance sheet:

1) Be owed to an outside party.

2) Be a result of a past transaction (an event has occurred to create the debt.)

3) Be repaid with an asset (normally cash.)

The major advantage of borrowing money to raise funds is that current ownership is not shared with new owners. The major disadvantage is the funds have to be repaid in the future and the associated cost of interest reduces earnings. Borrowing money is not a negative thing if the company earns more from using the money than the cost to use the money (called interest) and generates enough profit to repay the amount owed. The cost of interest on the borrowing and the terms of repayment are negotiated between the borrower and the lender.

The account name on the balance sheet indicates the general source of the funds. Common names used for different types of liabilities are described below:

Accounts Payable

The amount owed to suppliers is called accounts payable. Suppliers provide goods and services to a company repeatedly (normally monthly.)

An accounts payable occurs when the company does not pay at the time the goods or services are received. The company receives an invoice (bill) and normally has 30 days to pay what is owed, without interest. This is referred to as purchasing "on account."

Accounts payable decreases when the company pays the supplier.

Commercial Paper

Amounts owed to investors that must be repaid in less than a year is called commercial paper. The borrowed money is generally used to purchase inventory or pay operating expenses. Interest is charged at a very low rate because the money is borrowed for a short period of time. Only very large companies with strong credit ratings are allowed to borrow short-term from investors.

A company normally repays the investor by borrowing from another investor and does not use cash on hand to repay amounts owed.

14

Notes Payable

Amounts owed to banks and other financing companies expected to be repaid **within one year or less** are called **short-term notes payable**.

Amounts owed to banks and other financing companies expected to be repaid sometime **after one year** are called **long-term notes payable.**

Long-term Debt

Long-term debt means the same thing as long-term notes payable.

Current Maturities of Long-term Debt or Current Maturities of Notes Payable

The portion of long-term debt or long-term notes payable that must be repaid within one year is called current maturities of long-term debt or current maturities of notes payable.

Companies that repay debt with periodic payments (monthly or quarterly) repay a portion of the debt within one year and the rest of the debt is repaid after one year. An example of this is a five year car loan that must be repaid in monthly payments.

Bonds Payable

Borrowing from long-term investors in the public debt market (similar to a stock market for debt) is called bonds payable. The lender charges interest to the borrower (the company.)

Amounts due within a year or less are reported as current maturities of long-term debt. Bonds payable is sometimes referred to as notes payable on the balance sheet.

Interest on Notes Payable, Long-term Debt, and Bonds Payable

The company is charged interest on the amount owed for all long-term borrowings. The amount on the balance sheet for the borrowing represents the principle amount only and does not include interest.

The cost of using the money is reported on the income statement as interest expense. The amounts owed for interest that will be paid in the future is reported separately under the account name interest payable.

Example 2-2 presents a balance sheet for a company that has obtained funds to establish the business. No borrowings have been repaid as of the balance sheet date. The name on the balance sheet indicates the type of debt that is owed.

Assets:		Liabilities:	
Cash	$500,000	Short-term Notes Payable	$ 50,000
		Current Maturities of Long-term Notes Payable	$ 30,000
		Total Current Liabilities	$ 80,000
		Long-term Notes Payable	$170,000
		Bonds Payable	$240,000
		Total Liabilities	$490,000
		Stockholders' Equity:	
		Common Stock and Capital	$ 10,000
Total Assets	$500,000	Total Liabilities & Stockholders' Equity	$500,000

This company obtained $500,000 in cash to operate the business from the following sources:

1) The company borrowed $50,000 from a bank or financing institution that must be repaid in one year or less; short-term notes payable.

2) The company borrowed $200,000 from a bank or financing institution; $30,000 must be repaid in one year or less (current maturities of long-term notes payable) and $170,000 must be repaid in more than one year (long-term notes payable.)

3) The company borrowed $240,000 from investors that must be repaid in more than one year.

4) The owners contributed $10,000 to the company in exchange for common stock and capital (ownership.)

16

Money obtained from investors (owners) and creditors (lenders) is used to purchase items necessary to operate the business. Items the company uses to operate the business are called **assets**. An asset reported on the balance sheet must have **all three** of the following characteristics:

      1) Provide probable future economic benefit.

      2) Be owned or controlled by the company.

      3) Be a result of a past transaction.

Probable **future** economic benefit occurs when the asset is sold for cash or is used to generate revenues that will be received in cash in a future period. An asset is reported on the balance sheet when the item is expected to be used to provide goods or services to customers (generate economic benefit) or be exchanged for cash in future periods.

An asset that is no longer available to be used is removed from the balance sheet and reported on the income statement as an expense.

Costs that do not provide **future** economic benefit (generally because the benefit was received in the current period) are reported as expenses on the income statement.

A cost is either reported on the balance sheet as an asset or on the income statement as an expense. Assets used to do business will eventually be reported as an expense when the asset is used.

Assets do not reduce net earnings. Expenses reduce net earnings. The income statement is significantly impacted by the timing of when costs are reported as expenses. This concept is discussed in detail in chapter 5.

Cash

Money or any instrument that banks will accept for deposit in a company's account is considered cash. Examples of other instruments are checks, money orders and bank drafts.

Cash Equivalents

Investments that will be converted to cash within three months or less, with a market value not expected to change if interest rates change (no risk of loss), are considered cash equivalents. Examples of cash equivalents are certificates of deposit, treasury bills and commercial paper.

The company allows another entity use its excess cash in return for earning more cash (interest income.) Certificates of deposit represent money used by a bank. Treasury bills represent money used by the government. Commercial paper represents money used by other companies.

Investments and Marketable Securities

An investment occurs when a company uses excess cash to purchase a financial instrument (typically stocks or bonds) to earn a return. The company becomes an owner of another company when an investment in stock is made. The company becomes the lender to another entity when an investment in bonds is made. There are many types of available investments with different levels of risk and different amounts of expected return.

Investments decrease when a company sells the investment for cash.

Investments and marketable securities are classified as either **short-term** (one year or less) or **long-term** (more than one year) depending on how long the company intends to hold the investment.

Investments and marketable securities are different from cash equivalents because they carry a risk that the money invested will be lost. Cash equivalents have a history of returning the total amount invested.

Inventory

Items held only for sale to customers are called inventory.

Inventory increases when a company purchases or manufactures goods to sell to customers. Inventory decreases when the company provides goods to customers.

Supplies

Supplies are items used up in day to day operations. Supplies can be office supplies, paper products, glue, screws, or any small dollar items that must be consistently replaced.

Prepaid Expenses

Amounts a company pays in for services that will be provided to the company in the future are called prepaid expenses.

> Examples: Insurance paid on January 1st for six months of coverage is considered prepaid for the next six months that have not yet passed.
>
> Rent paid on January 1st for the month of January is considered prepaid for the days in January that have not yet passed.

Prepaid expenses generally decrease as time passes.

Notes Receivable and Financing Receivables

Notes receivable represents amounts owed to a company. The company loans money to another party (another company or employees) and expects to be repaid over a period of time. Interest is charged to the borrower by the company and the company earns interest income.

Financing receivables represent amounts owed to a company for financing the purchase of goods or services for customers. Customers agree to pay for the goods or services over a period of time. Interest is charged to the customer and the company earns interest income. An example of a financing receivable is Dell, Inc. sales computers to customers who agree to pay Dell for the computer with monthly payments that include interest for three years. Dell will report the amounts owed from customers as a financing receivable.

Notes or financing receivables includes only the principle amount expected to be received from others. Interest earned is not included in the amount of the notes or financing receivable. Interest earned that has not been received is called interest receivable and is reported separately.

Notes and financing receivables can be **short-term** (one year or less) or **long-term** (more than one year) depending on when the company expects to be repaid.

Property, Plant and Equipment

Items used for more than one year to provide goods or services to customers are called property, plant, and equipment. Property, plant, and equipment have **physical substance** and include such things as land, buildings, manufacturing equipment, furniture and fixtures, computers, equipment, and vehicles.

Intangible Assets

Intangible assets give the company the exclusive right to do something for more than one year. Intangible assets have **no** physical substance.

Examples of different types of intangible assets are as follows:

<u>Trademarks</u> give the exclusive right from the U.S. Government to use a symbol or name.

<u>Copyrights</u> give the exclusive right from the U.S. Government to reproduce written work.

<u>Patents</u> give the exclusive right from the U.S. Government to use a new innovation. Patents are granted to protect an invention from imitators.

<u>Franchises</u> give the exclusive right to sell a specific branded product from the owner of a branded product.

<u>Goodwill</u> is the amount paid to acquire a company above the fair market value of the net assets acquired. The amount paid is more than the total fair market value of net assets purchased because the business is established and has the ability to generate more future cash flows than the separate individual assets.

> The amount paid for the entire company
> - The fair market value of net assets acquired
> = Goodwill

Goodwill consists of a good management team, a good location, and name brand recognition developed over time as the business grows. Goodwill makes the individual assets worth more when used together with the intangible factors.

Goodwill must be **purchased** to be reported on the balance sheet. Internally generated goodwill is not reported on the balance sheet because no exchange occurs and it is difficult to value objectively.

Example 2-3 illustrates how goodwill is reported on the balance sheet. Bop, Inc. purchases Yip, Inc. for $500,000. The fair market value of the identifiable assets acquired as part of the purchase is $220,000. Bop, Inc. agreed to repay $100,000 of liabilities owed by Yip, Inc.

The amount paid for the entire company	$500,000
+ The amount of liabilities assumed in the purchase	$100,000
- The fair market value of assets purchased	($220,000)
= Goodwill	$380,000

The balance sheet for Bop, Inc. will report $500,000 less cash, additional assets as identified (such as inventory, equipment, trademarks, etc.) for $220,000, goodwill for $380,000, and additional liabilities of $100,000 after the purchase.

Other Long-term Assets

Assets held for more than one year which do not fit into other asset categories are reported as other long-term assets. Examples include long-term assets that are currently not being used and the cash value of life insurance policies.

Stockholders' Equity

Stockholders' equity of a company is very similar to the equity of a homeowner. A house purchased at a cost of $100,000 with a loan in the amount of $85,000 and a cash payment of $15,000 from the owner is reported on a balance sheet as follows:

Assets:		Liabilities:	
House	$100,000 (cost)	Notes Payable	$85,000 (borrowed)
		Stockholders' Equity:	
		Stock	$15,000 (owners)

The owners of the house contributed $15,000 and borrowed $85,000 and purchased the $100,000 house. The $100,000 cost of the house less the amount of $85,000 owed equals $15,000 "equity" in the home. In the same way, a company's stockholders' equity is the net of the total assets and total liabilities of the company.

Stockholders' equity primarily consists of the following two parts:

1) Financing provided by owners (stock and capital.)
2) Earnings retained in the company.

The cash and earnings provided by the owners, along with funds obtained from borrowing, are used to purchase assets to operate the business.

Stock and Capital

Financing provided by owners is reported as **stock and capital.** Capital is also called capital in excess of par, additional paid in capital, or contributed capital.

The amount of stock reported on the balance sheet is the **par value** of one share multiplied by the number of shares of stock issued to investors. Par value is an arbitrary amount stated in the articles of incorporation that represents the legal capital requirements of the corporation. Par value is typically set at a very small amount and does <u>not</u> represent the fair market value of the stock.

21

Example 2-4 illustrates how funds received from owners in exchange for shares of stock are reported on the balance sheet.

The company issued 5,000 shares of common stock with a par value of $0.10 per share in exchange for $10,000.

The balance sheet will report the following:

Stock	$ 500	5,000 shares x $0.10 par
Capital	$ 9,500	$10,000 total received less total par value

The value reported for stock is equal to the number of shares issued multiplied by par value. The value reported for capital is the difference in total cash received and the total par value of the stock issued.

Financing provided by owners is reported on the balance sheet as **stock and capital.** Capital is also referred to as capital in excess of par, paid in capital, additional paid in capital and contributed capital. <u>Both accounts</u> are used when cash is contributed by owners. The two accounts together equal the total amount received from owners.

The two types of stock typically issued by corporations are **common stock** and **preferred stock.** Common stock has voting rights. Investors in common stock generally desire appreciation of value or the ability to influence operations. Preferred stock has no voting rights and is purchased by investors to earn a consistent return on their investment at the stated interest rate.

The maximum number of shares a corporation can issue is referred to as shares **authorized.** The total number of shares that have been sold to investors to date is referred to as **issued** shares. Shares owned by stockholders other than the corporation are referred to as **outstanding** shares.

Dividends are considered a return of the investment by owners and are not reported as an expense on the income statement. Dividends reduce retained earnings.

All dividends paid to owners must be authorized by the board of directors. A dividend is **declared** when the board of directors promises a payment to owners. Retained earnings is reduced when dividends are declared. Dividends are generally paid approximately ten to forty-five days after the dividend is declared. A liability is reported until the dividend is paid.

Dividends are not required to be paid if the board of directors decides the funds should be kept in the business and used for other purposes.

Retained Earnings

Retained earnings is the total cumulative earnings of the company less all amounts returned to stockholders to date since the first day of operations. The amount reported on the balance sheet for retained earnings is computed as follows:

> Retained Earnings, at the beginning of the year (prior year ending balance)
> + Current year earnings; reported on the income statement
> - Dividends declared to stockholders during the current year
> = Retained Earnings, at the end of the year (reported on the balance sheet)

Example 2-5 illustrates how retained earnings for PepsiCo. Inc. changed from December 31, 2010 to December 31, 2011.

Retained earnings on December 31, 2010	$37,090
+ Earnings during the year ended December 31, 2011	$ 6,443
- Dividends declared to stockholders during 2011	(\$ 3,217)
= Retained earnings on December 31, 2011	$40,316

Treasury Stock

Treasury Stock is the amount the company has paid to purchase and hold the company's own stock. Companies purchase their own stock to demonstrate confidence in future performance, to reduce the number of outstanding shares, or to sell to employees at a later date.

Common stock represents all shares that have been issued. Treasury stock is common stock that is owned by the company rather than investors outside the company. Treasury stock is also issued common stock.   It is reported separately because it is owned by the company.

Common Shares	100,000	Total shares issued to all owners
- Treasury Shares	(5,000)	Shares owned by the company
= Outstanding Shares	95,000	Shares owned by outsiders

Total stockholders' equity represents the amount owned by owners outside the company. **Treasury shares are negative** to show the reduction to the amount owned by owners outside the company.

Other Comprehensive Income

Other comprehensive income consists of gains or losses that are not reported on the income statement, yet. The gains and losses are reported as part of stockholders' equity until the time comes to report the amount on the income statement (according to accounting rules). Examples of items reported in other comprehensive income are gains and losses related to foreign currency, gains and losses related to certain types of investments and derivatives, and items related to employee pensions.

Accounting guidance related to other comprehensive income is very complex and is beyond the scope of this book.

The Classified Balance Sheet

Financial accounting guidance requires the balance sheet to be presented in a common format referred to as a classified balance sheet. The balance sheet sorts and subtotals the assets and liabilities into groups based on **liquidity**. Liquidity is determined by how soon an asset is expected to convert into cash or a liability is expected to be paid. Cash is more liquid than inventory which is more liquid than equipment.

It is important for users of the balance sheet to know when assets are expected to be converted into cash and when liabilities are required to be repaid. The balance sheet subtotals **short-term or current** accounts that are expected to be used or exchanged for cash (assets) or repaid (liabilities) in **one year or less** and groups **non-current or long-term** accounts that are expected to be used (assets) or repaid (liabilities) in **more than one year.** The following categories are presented on the balance sheet:

> **Current Assets** includes all assets expected to be used or collected in cash within one year or less.

> **Property, plant and equipment** includes all physical assets expected to be used for more than one year.

> **Intangible assets** include all non-physical assets expected to be used for more than one year.

> **Current liabilities** includes all amounts owed that are expected to be paid within one year or less.

> **Long-term Liabilities** includes all amounts owed that are expected to be paid in more than one year.

Sorting and subtotaling allows for easy comparison of a company's financial position to other companies. It also provides the information necessary for financial analysis (discussed in chapter 10.)

24

Example 2-6 presents a classified balance sheet of a company that has obtained money from investors and creditors and used the money to purchase items to operate the business.
This balance sheet reports the company's financial position <u>before</u> the company provides goods and services to customers.

ABC, Inc.
Balance Sheet
As of a Particular Date

Assets:		Liabilities:	
Cash and Cash Equivalents	10,000	Accounts Payable	9,000
Inventory	42,000	Short-term Notes Payable	30,000
Supplies	1,000	Current Maturities of Long-term Debt	40,000
Prepaid Expenses	3,000		
Short-term Investments	25,000	**Total Current Liabilities**	**79,000**
Total Current Assets	**81,000**		
Long-term Investments	50,000	Long-term Debt	200,000
Long-term Notes Receivable	15,000	Bonds Payable	400,000
		Total Liabilities	**679,000**
Property, Plant, and Equipment:			
Land	100,000		
Buildings	300,000		
Furniture and Fixtures	62,000		
Equipment	95,000		
Vehicles	43,000		
Total Property, Plant, and Equipment	**600,000**		
		Stockholders' Equity:	
Intangible Assets		Common Stock and Capital	200,000
Goodwill	88,000		
Patents	12,000		
Copyrights	6,000	**Total Stockholders' Equity**	**200,000**
Trademarks	11,000		
Total Intangible Assets	**117,000**		
Other Long-term Assets	16,000		
		Total Liabilities &	
Total Assets	**879,000**	**Stockholders' Equity**	**879,000**

Total assets must equal total liabilities plus stockholders' equity. A company either owns or owes for all assets used to operate the business. Total funds to purchase assets must come either from borrowings or from the owners.

All items reported on the balance sheet must meet the accounting definition of an asset, liability, or stockholders' equity defined previously in this chapter.

The balance sheet does not state the transactions that were done to change the assets and liabilities. The balance sheet states items used by the company to do business and amounts owed by the company **on the specified date.**

Assets on the balance sheet are initially reported at historical cost. Historical cost is the amount paid for the asset. An asset can be paid for with cash when purchased, paid for with cash in a future period, or purchased with the exchange of another asset.

Example 2-7 illustrates how to determine historical cost. A company gave equipment valued at $12,000, gave cash of $20,000, and agrees to pay $8,000 over the next 5 years, to purchase a delivery truck.

The historical cost of the truck is $40,000. Historical cost is the total of all amounts exchanged for the asset. ($12,000 + $20,000 + $8,000 = $40,000)

Amounts are initially reported on the balance sheet at historical cost because historical cost can be verified. There are times that reporting the amounts at fair market value may be more useful to a user making an investment decision; however, fair market value is often subjective opinion that is difficult to verify.

Users of financial information have decided that amounts that can be verified are better information to use for decision making than amounts that are based on subjective opinion.

Amount may be reported at fair market value when the amount can be verified. This occurs with investments that are traded on a public exchange with a quoted fair market value.

Amounts will be reported at less than cost when the cost of the asset is higher than the expected probable future economic benefit from the asset. Assets cannot be reported at an amount higher than the expected probable future economic benefit from using the assets.

For example, a machine that cost $100,000 that is expected to be used to produce products that can be sold for net cash of $80,000 will be reported at $80,000. The $80,000 future economic benefit of using the machine is lower than the cost of $100,000. The machine cannot be reported at higher than its expected probable future economic benefit. This will be discussed further in chapter 5.

Example 2-8 presents the balance sheet for Best Buy, Inc., a retailer of electronics. Accounts that have not been discussed in this chapter are replaced with XXXXXXXX. These accounts will be discussed in chapter 6. The numbers before the account names relate to the explanations on the next page and are not reported on the actual balance sheet of Best Buy, Inc.

Best Buy, Inc.
Consolidated Balance Sheets
$ in millions, except per share and share amounts

	February 26, 2011	February 27, 2010
Assets		
Current Assets		
(1) Cash and cash equivalents	$ 1,103	$ 1,826
(2) Short-term investments	22	90
(3) Merchandise inventories	5,897	5,486
XXXXXXXXXX	3,451	3,164
(11) **Total current assets**	10,473	10,566
(4) **Net property and equipment**	3,823	4,070
(5) **Goodwill**	2,454	2,452
(6) **Trade names, Net**	133	159
XXXXXXXXXXXXX	966	1,055
Total Assets	$ 17,849	$ 18,302
Liabilities		
(7) Accounts payable	$ 4,894	$ 5,276
XXXXXXXXXXXXXXX	2,771	3,004
(7) Short-term debt	557	663
(8) Current portion of long-term debt	441	35
(11) **Total current liabilities**	8,663	8,978
(8) **Long-term Debt**	711	1,104
XXXXXXXXXXXXXX	1,183	1,256
Total Liabilities	10,557	11,338
Equity		
(9) Common stock, $0.10 par value: Authorized — 1.0 billion shares; Issued and outstanding — 392,590,000 and 418,815,000 shares, respectively	39	42
(9) Additional Paid in Capital	881	1,125
(10) Retained earnings	6,372	5,797
Total equity	7,292	6,964
Total Liabilities and Equity	$ 17,849	$ 18,302

Example 2-8 continued

Notice the following on the balance sheet for Best Buy, Inc.:

1) The company reports cash in the bank together with cash equivalents. These are considered the same type of asset since cash equivalents have a minimal risk of loss.

2) The company has invested a small amount of cash in investments with a risk of loss. Short-term investments are intended to be held for one year or less.

3) The largest asset the company has is merchandise inventories held for sale to customers.

4) The company has property and equipment that is expected to be used more than one year to operate the business. The footnotes state the company owns warehouse equipment, store fixtures, and computer systems. The net amount reported is historical cost less the cost of using the assets for all periods the assets have been used. The net amount represents the estimated cost of using the property and equipment in the future and does not represent fair market value.

5) Goodwill indicates Best Buy, Inc. has purchased other companies in prior years. No change in the amount from 2010 to 2011 indicates no companies were purchased in 2011. The amount of goodwill is the amount paid over and above the fair market value of the identifiable net assets purchased when buying another company.

6) The amount for trade names, net is the cost of acquiring the trade names less the cost of using them for all periods used. The net amount represents the cost allocated to future use and does not represent the fair market value of the trade names.

7) The company owes amounts that must be repaid in less than one year. Accounts payable is owed to suppliers and short-term debt is owed to banks or financing institutions. Accounts payable is listed first, indicating that it is expected to be paid before any other amounts owed.

8) Long-term debt indicates the company has borrowed money from banks, financing institutions, or investors. The amount that must be paid in one year or less is reported as current portion of long-term debt. The amount that must be paid later than one year is reported as long-term debt.

9) Owners have paid the company a total of $920 million in return for ownership. This is reported as common stock at par of $39 million and additional paid in capital of $881 million.

10) The company has earned and kept in the business over $6.3 billion since operations began. This amount has been reinvested in the business instead of returned as dividends to owners.

11) Total current assets of $10,473 are larger than total current liabilities of $8,663. This indicates the company should have enough cash and assets to repay liabilities associated with day to day operations and repay debt due within one year. The ability to pay is dependent on timely sales of inventory and collection of cash from customers.

Example 2-9 presents the balance sheet for PepsiCo, Inc., a manufacturer and distributor of food and beverages. Items that have not been discussed in this chapter are replaced with XXXXXXXX. These accounts will be discussed in chapter 6. The numbers before the account names relate to the explanations on the next page and are not stated on PepsiCo Inc.'s actual balance sheet.

PepsiCo, Inc. BALANCE SHEETS

(In millions)

June 30,		2010		2009
Assets				
Current assets:				
(1) Cash and cash equivalents	$	5,943	$	3,943
(1) Short-term investments		426		192
(2) Inventories		3,372		2,618
XXXXXXXXXXXXX		7,828		5,818
Total current assets		17,569		12,571
(3) Property, plant, and equipment, net		19,058		12,671
Investments		1,368		4,484
(4) Goodwill		14,661		6,534
(5) Intangible assets, net		13,808		2,623
(6) Other long-term assets		1,689		965
Total assets	$	68,153	$	39,848
Liabilities and stockholders' equity				
(7) Accounts payable and other	$	10,923	$	8,127
(7) Short-term obligations		4,898		464
XXXXXXXXXXXXXX		71		165
Total current liabilities		15,892		8,756
(8) Long-term debt		19,999		7,400
XXXXXXXXXXXX		10,776		6,250
Total liabilities		46,677		22,406
Commitments and contingencies				
Stockholders' equity:				
(9) Stock and paid-in capital		4,449		176
(10) Retained Earnings		37,090		33,805
(11) Treasury Stock		(16,745)		(13,383)
(12) Accumulated other comprehensive income		(3,630)		(3,794)
XXXXXXXXXX		312		638
Total Stockholder's equity		21,476		17,442
Total liabilities and stockholders' equity		68,153		39,848

Example 2-9 continued:

Notice the following on the balance sheet for PepsiCo, Inc.:

1) The company has almost $6 billion of cash in the bank or invested in cash equivalents. Short-term investments are intended to be held for one year or less and have a risk of loss.

2) The amount of inventory for sale to customers is about $3.4 billion.

3) The company has property, plant, and equipment used to manufacture inventory and operate the business. The footnotes report that approximately 70% of property, plant and equipment is machinery and equipment. The net amount reported on the balance sheet is the estimated cost using the property, plant, and equipment in the future. The amount does not represent fair market value.

4) The significant increase in goodwill indicates PepsiCo, Inc. purchased other companies during 2010. Goodwill is the amount paid over and above the fair value of the net assets purchased when buying other companies. The footnotes state the following: On February 26, 2010, we completed our acquisitions of The Pepsi Bottling Group, Inc. and PepsiAmericas, Inc.

5) PepsiCo, Inc. has intangible assets that give the company exclusive rights. The amount reported on the balance sheet is the cost paid for the intangible assets less the total estimated cost of using the intangible assets to date. The amount does not represent fair market value.

6) Other long-term assets include items the company owns that do not belong in any other asset category. The amount is not significant to total assets and no detail is provided.

7) PepsiCo, Inc. owes suppliers who must be paid in approximately 30 days. Short-term obligations must be repaid in one year or less. The footnotes report short-term obligations consist of approximately $1.6 billion in current maturities of long term debt and approximately $2.6 billion owed for commercial paper.

8) The company has borrowed money from banks, financing institutions, or investors. The amount owed must be paid sometime after one year. The increase from 2009 to 2010 was significant.

9) The over $4 billion increase in stock and paid-in-capital from 2009 to 2010 indicates contributions were made by owners. The funds from owners, along with the additional funds obtained from borrowing long-term debt (8), were used to purchase The Pepsi Bottling Group, Inc. and PepsiAmericas, Inc.

10) PepsiCo, Inc. has reinvested earnings of $37,090 since operations began.

11) Treasury stock is PepsiCo, Inc. common stock that is owned by PepsiCo, Inc. The increase indicates the company purchased more of its own stock in 2010. The amount reported is the purchase cost and does not represent fair market value.

12) Accumulated other comprehensive income consists of losses that may be reported on the income statement in future years.

3. Things that Change the Balance Sheet

The balance sheet states what the company uses to operate the business, amounts owed and how much is owned by stockholders **as of a certain date**. It is common for the balance sheet to report amounts for two different dates for comparison; such as December 31, 2010 and December 31, 2011. The balance sheet does not report the specific transactions that occur to change the amount of an item from one date to another date.

A **transaction** is anything a business does which results in an exchange of one item for another item. The following common transactions change the amounts reported on the balance sheet:

1) Assets increase when purchased and decrease when sold.

2) Liabilities increase when funds are borrowed and decrease when debts are repaid.

3) Stockholder's equity changes when funds are exchanged between the company and the owners and with profits and losses.

The amounts on the balance sheet for assets represent the <u>cumulative cost</u> (or expected future benefit) of the assets owned on the date of the balance sheet.

The amounts on the balance sheet for liabilities represents <u>cumulative amounts owed</u> on the date of the balance sheet.

It is the accountant's responsibility to call things the company has and owes by a name that is generally recognized by the reader of the balance sheet. The names commonly used are called **accounts.** The accounts reported on the balance sheet were discussed in chapter 2.

Accounting is called a double entry system because a minimum of two accounts change with each transaction. A transaction is an exchange of one thing for another; therefore, at least two things must always change.

The following questions should be answered to determine how the balance sheet will change with a given transaction:

      1) What does the company <u>have</u> more or less of? **Changes <u>assets</u>; which account?**

      2) Does the company <u>owe</u> more or less? **Changes <u>liabilities</u>; which account?**

      3) Was there an exchange that involved the <u>owners</u>? **Changes <u>stockholders' equity</u>;**
                                                  which account?

Remember the following:

      1) an asset is something owned or used to operate the business.

      2) a liability is an amount owed that must be paid in the future.

      3) stockholders' equity is equal to total assets less total liabilities.

Assets are purchased with cash contributed by owners or cash borrowed.   Assets are either <u>owned</u> or were purchased with <u>debt.</u> The balance sheet represents this fact in the form of the **accounting equation.**

The left side of the equation represents what the company uses to operate the business and the right side of the equation represents how the company purchased the assets (with debt or cash from owners.)

Assets	=	**Liabilities**	+	**Stockholders' Equity**
Have		Owe		Own (includes earnings)

The accounting equation will always stay in balance when a transaction occurs. Both sides of the equation do not have to change. A transaction that changes two accounts on one side of the equation will net to zero and the other side of the equation will not change.

There are four common transactions that occur repeatedly as a business operates. The most common transactions that change the accounts and amounts reported on the balance sheet and the accounting equation are as follows:

1) Receive cash from investors (owners.)

Assets	=	Liabilities	+	Stockholders' Equity
Have more	=		+	Own more

2) Trade one asset for another asset (often paying cash for another asset.)

Assets	=	Liabilities	+	Stockholders' Equity
Have more	=		+	
and have less				

3) Receive an asset and pay for the asset in the future (liability.)

Assets	=	Liabilities	+	Stockholders' Equity
Have more	=	Owe more	+	

4) Pay cash to reduce amounts owed (liability.)

Assets	=	Liabilities	+	Stockholders' Equity
Have less	=	Owe less	+	

Example 3-1 demonstrates how the three questions are used to identify the things that change on the balance sheet when a transaction occurs. The accountant determines the account names that change, records the amount, and summarizes the total results of all transactions. This information is used to prepare the balance sheet at the end of the period.

Example 3-1: Pillow Soft, Inc. sells pillows to retailers. The company had the following business transactions during the first month the business was established. Each transaction changes the balance sheet.

1. The company sold 100 shares of common stock for $2,000 per share for a total of $200,000.

      The company received cash and gave ownership to others outside the company.

      1) What does the company <u>have</u> more or less of? **More cash; $200,000**

      2) Does the company <u>owe</u> more or less? **No**

      3) Was there an exchange that involved the owners? **Yes,** the owners put money into the company in exchange for ownership;

                                                More common stock; $200,000

2. Paid $6,000 cash for the first three months rent of the warehouse and office facility.

      The company paid cash for the right to use the facility for the <u>next</u> three months.

      The right to use the facility for three months is a future economic benefit (asset.) One asset was traded for another asset.

      1) What does the company <u>have</u> more or less of? **Less cash; $6,000**
                                                      More prepaid rent; $6,000

      2) Does the company <u>owe</u> more or less? **No**

      3) Was there an exchange that involved the owners? **No**

3. Purchased warehouse equipment for $50,000 cash.

      The company received warehouse equipment in exchange for cash.
      The warehouse equipment will be used to generate future economic benefit.

      1) What does the company <u>have</u> more or less of? **Less cash; $50,000**
                                                More warehouse equipment; $50,000

      2) Does the company <u>owe</u> more or less? **No**

      3) Was there an exchange that involved the owners? **No**

4. Purchased office furniture for $15,000 cash.

The company received office furniture in exchange for cash.
The office furniture will be used to generate future economic benefit.

1) What does the company <u>have</u> more or less of? **Less cash; $15,000**
More office furniture; $15,000

2) Does the company <u>owe</u> more or less? **No**

3) Was there an exchange that involved the owners? **No**

5. Purchased computer equipment (hardware and software) for $18,000 cash.

The company received computer equipment in exchange for cash.
The computer equipment will be used to generate future economic benefit.

1) What does the company <u>have</u> more or less of? **Less cash; $18,000**
More computer equipment; $18,000

2) Does the company <u>owe</u> more or less? **No**

3) Was there an exchange that involved the owners? **No**

6. Paid $12,000 cash for six months of future insurance coverage.

The company exchanged cash for insurance coverage for the <u>next</u> six months.
Insurance coverage paid for before the service is provided is a future economic
benefit (an asset.)

1) What does the company <u>have</u> more or less of? **Less cash; $12,000**
More prepaid insurance; $12,000

2) Does the company <u>owe</u> more or less? **No**

3) Was there an exchange that involved the owners? **No**

7. Purchased goods to sell to customers for $60,000 on account (pay in 30 days.)

The company received inventory and agreed to pay the supplier in the future.

1) What does the company <u>have</u> more or less of?   **More inventory; $60,000**

2) Does the company <u>owe</u> more or less? **Yes, more accounts payable; $60,000**

3) Was there an exchange that involved the owners? **No**

8. Purchased office supplies to be used during the year for $300, on account.

The office supplies were not paid for at the time of the purchase.
  The company owes the supplier.

1) What does the company <u>have</u> more or less of?   **More office supplies; $300**

2) Does the company <u>owe</u> more or less? **Yes, more accounts payable; $300**

3) Was there an exchange that involved the owners? **No**

9. Borrowed $25,000 from the bank. $5,000 must be repaid at the end of every year for five years.

The company received cash and agreed to pay in the future.

1) What does the company <u>have</u> more or less of?   **More cash; $25,000**

2) Does the company <u>owe</u> more or less? **Yes, more notes payable**
        $5,000 is Current Maturities of Long-term Notes Payable
        $20,000 is Long-term Notes Payable

3) Was there an exchange that involved the owners? **No**

The accountant records what occurred with each transaction and prepares the balance sheet to show what the company **has** (assets), **owes** (liabilities), and **owns** (stockholders' equity) at the end of the period, the first month of operations.   A simple spreadsheet is used to record what happened. Every account name used, along with the total net amount, is reported on the balance sheet. The spreadsheet on the next page illustrates how Pillow Soft, Inc.'s transactions during the first month of business are recorded.

Assets

	Cash	Inventory	Prepaid Rent	Prepaid Insurance	Office Supplies	Warehouse Equipment
1)	$200,000					
2)	($6,000)		$6,000			
3)	($50,000)					$50,000
4)	($15,000)					
5)	($18,000)					
6)	($12,000)			$12,000		
7)		$60,000				
8)					$300	
9)	$ 25,000					
Total	**$124,000**	**$60,000**	**$6,000**	**$12,000**	**$300**	**$50,000**

Assets   =   Liabilities   +   Equity

	Office Furniture	Computer Equipment	Accounts Payable	CM notes Payable	L/T Notes Payable	Common Stock and Capital
1)						$200,000
2)						
3)						
4)	$15,000					
5)		$18,000				
6)						
7)			$60,000			
8)			$ 300			
9)				$5,000	$20,000	
Total	**$15,000**	**$18,000**	**$60,300**	**$5,000**	**$20,000**	**$200,000**

Total Assets $285,300 = Total Liabilities $85,300 + Total Stockholders' Equity $200,000

Accounts are placed on the balance sheet under the proper category: assets, liabilities, or stockholders' equity. The account names are listed in order of liquidity. The totals for each account are placed beside the name of the account to quantify the amounts the company has, owes, or owns.

Pillow Soft, Inc.'s classified balance sheet as of January 31st, will report the following:

Assets:		Liabilities:	
Cash	$124,000	Accounts Payable	$60,300
Inventory	60,000	Current Maturities of	
Prepaid Rent	6,000	Notes Payable	$ 5,000
Prepaid Insurance	12,000	Total Current Liabilities	$65,300
Office Supplies	300		
Total Current Assets	202,300	Long-term Notes Payable	$20,000
		Total Liabilities	$85,300
Property, Plant, & Equipment:		Stockholders' Equity:	
Warehouse Equipment	50,000		
Office Furniture	15,000	Common Stock	
Computer Equipment	18,000	and Capital	200,000
Total Prop., Plant, Equip.	83,000		
		Total Liabilities &	
Total Assets	$285,300	Stockholders' Equity	$285,300

The <u>assets</u> listed report that on January 31st, the date of the balance sheet, the company
    1) has cash in the bank of $124,000.
    2) has inventory that cost $60,000 that is expected to be sold to customers.
    3) paid for rent and insurance <u>before</u> the space is used and the coverage is provided.
    4) has office supplies that cost $300 that will be used in the next year.
    5) has warehouse equipment, office furniture and computer equipment that cost
       a total of $83,000. They will be used more than one year to operate the business.

All assets (other than cash) will either be exchanged for cash or will be used to operate the business and generate future economic benefit, ultimately more cash.

<u>Liabilities</u> are amounts <u>owed</u> to others. The company owes $60,300 to suppliers for purchases on account. The accounts payable will be paid within 30 to 60 days. Notes payable is owed to banks and financing institutions; a portion of the amount owed will be repaid in the next year.

<u>Stockholders' equity</u> represents <u>ownership</u> by outside investors. Investors have contributed $200,000 to the company in exchange for ownership (common stock and capital.)

Total stockholders' equity equals total assets less total liabilities.

4. The Income Statement

The income statement reports the earnings of the company <u>for a specific period of time.</u>

A business operates to provide goods or services to customers at a higher price to the customer (revenues) than it costs the business to provide the goods or services (expenses.) The company's performance is measured as the difference in the value provided to customers and the cost to provide the goods or services to the customer. The net result of revenues less expenses is called net earnings or net income.

Revenues occur when a company provides goods or services <u>to customers</u> in return for an asset (normally cash or a promise to receive cash in the future.)

> Revenue is reported on the income statement during the period it is **earned.**
> Revenue is considered to be **earned** when the following two things occur:
>
> > 1) Delivery of goods has occurred or a service has been provided to the customer and nothing more is owed to the customer.
> >
> > **and**
> >
> > 2) The company expects to receive an asset (payment is reasonably assured.)
>
> **Important:** Revenue occurs when goods or services are provided to a customer who is expected to pay for the goods or services, **<u>not</u>** when cash is collected from the customer.

Expenses are reported on the income statement during the period they are **incurred.**
An expense is considered to be **incurred** when the following occurs:

> > 1) A service is provided <u>to the company.</u>
> >
> > **or**
> >
> > 2) An asset is used (up) to provide goods or services to customers.
>
> **Important:** The expense is "incurred" when the company receives the service or the asset is used (up), **<u>not</u>** when the company pays cash for the service or asset.

Gains and losses from selling assets (other than inventory) are also reported on the income statement.

Gains occur when a company sells an asset and receives <u>more</u> than the asset's net cost.

Losses occur when a company sells an asset and receives <u>less</u> than the asset's net cost.

Companies sell property and equipment at the end of use. The difference in the net cost and cash received from the sale is the gain or loss. The gain or loss on investments is the difference in the cost of the investment and the cash received from the sale.

Gains and losses that are not related to the primary business of providing goods and services to customers are also reported on the income statement. Gains and losses can occur from lawsuits, environmental cleanups, and natural disasters such as tornados, hurricanes or floods.

Example 4-1: An income statement for a business that provides lawn care services would report the following:

Lawn Care, Inc. **Income Statement** **For the Year Ended 12/31/20XX**	**The line item means the following happened during 20XX:**
Service Revenue	Lawn services were provided to customers.
- Salary Expense	Employees provided services to the company.
- Gasoline Expense	The asset gasoline was used up.
- Depreciation Expense	Equipment was used to service customers.
- <u>Business Insurance Expense</u>	<u>Insurance coverage was provided to the company.</u>
= Income from Operations	Earnings for the year from daily operations.
+ Gain from Selling Investments	Investments were sold for > than reported value.
- <u>Loss from Fire</u>	<u>The net cost of assets lost in a fire.</u>
= Income Before Tax	Earnings before paying the government.
- <u>Income Tax Expense</u>	<u>The amount that must be paid to the government.</u>
= Net Income	Net earnings of the company for the year.

It is important to notice that everything reported on the income statement happened during the year ended December 31, 20XX (between January 1 and December 31, 20XX.) The income statement does **not** report the amount of cash collected or paid for each item listed.
The timing of **when cash is received or paid** is not considered when presenting items on the income statement.

Goods or services must be **provided to a customer <u>during the period</u>** for revenues to be reported on the income statement for the current period.

The following are examples of revenue during the current period:

1) Pillows are shipped to customers.
2) A heating and air conditioning company repairs a customer's air conditioning system.
3) A paint and body shop repairs a customer's auto.
4) Microsoft ships software to Dell Computer.
5) Google provides a search click to a customer and an internet user clicks on the ad.
6) A customer flies from Dallas to Orlando.

Goods or services were provided to a customer during the current period.

The following are NOT examples of revenues during the current period:

1) An order for pillows is received from customers.
2) A heating and air conditioning company schedules a repair of a customer's air conditioning system.
3) A paint and body shop accepts a check from an insurance company to repair a customer's auto and the repair will be done next month.
4) Microsoft agrees to ship software to Dell Computer over the next three months.
5) Google agrees to provide a search click for a customer and no clicks have occurred.
6) A flight for next month is reserved and paid for by a customer.

Goods or services have not yet been provided to a customer.

Expenses are reported on the income statement <u>in the period</u> **an asset is used (or used up) or a service is provided to the company.**

The following are examples of expenses during the current period:

1) Advertisements of the company's products appeared in a weekly magazine.
2) Employees worked for the company during the month.
3) The company is covered by an insurance company during the month.
4) Supplies were used up during the month.
5) Inventory is provided to customers during the month.
6) Equipment was used during the month.

Services were provided to the company or an asset was used (up) during the current period.

The following are NOT examples of expenses during the current period:

1) Advertisements are paid for and scheduled to be run next month in a weekly magazine.
2) Employees are hired and will begin work next month.
3) The company paid for insurance coverage to begin next month.
4) Supplies are purchased and have not been used.
5) Inventory is purchased and is in the warehouse.
6) Equipment was purchased and has not been used.

Services have not been provided to the company or assets have NOT been used (up.)

The following important things need to be remembered about the income statement:

The income statement generally reports two or three separate periods of time for comparison purposes. A period of time is normally a month, a quarter, or a year.

The income statement reports only what happened during the specified period of time reported. The event (goods or services provided to customers, use of an asset, or service provided to the company) must occur during the specified period to be reported on the income statement for that period of time.

Events are reported on the income statement when they occur, **not when cash** is received or paid. When cash is received or paid is not a concern of the income statement. It is common that cash is received or cash is paid in the same period the revenue is earned or the expense is incurred; however, the exchange of cash is not the reason the amount is reported during the period. The balance sheet reports when the exchange of cash occurs. This will be discussed further in chapter 6.

The income statement reports the following three types of things that happen during a specific period of time:

1) Goods or services were provided to the customer.   **Revenue**

2) An asset other than cash was used (or used up.) **Expense**

3) A service* was provided to the company.   **Expense**

* Note: Goods provided to the company are reported as assets on the balance sheet until the goods are no longer available to use.

Example 4-2 gives several transactions and demonstrates how three questions are used to determine if a transaction is reported on the <u>current period</u> income statement. This example also illustrates some of the common names reported on the income statement.

a. Cash was received from owners in exchange for ownership.

1) Goods or service provided to customers? NO
2) Service provided to the company? NO
3) Asset other than cash used (up)? NO

> Nothing is reported on the income statement.

b. Lawn equipment was used.

1) Goods or service provided to customers? NO
2) Service provided to the company? NO
3) Asset other than cash used (up)? Yes, using a long-term asset is called depreciation

> Depreciation expense is reported on the income statement.

c. Gasoline was used up.

1) Goods or service provided to customers? NO Consider only what is stated; do not assume that a service was provided when the gasoline was used.)
2) Service provided to the company? NO
3) Asset other than cash used (up)? YES, gasoline

> Gasoline expense is reported on the income statement.

d. Lawns were cut for customers.

1) Goods or service provided to customers? YES, lawn service revenue
2) Service provided to the company? NO
3) Asset other than cash used (up)? NO

> Lawn service revenue is reported on the income statement.

e. Supplies (weed eating twine, bags, grass squares) were purchased.

1) Goods or service provided to customers? NO
2) Service provided to the company? NO
3) Asset other than cash used (up)? NO, supplies are assets until the supplies are used

> Nothing is reported on the income statement until an asset is used.

Example 4-2 continued

f. Employees worked this period.

1) Goods or service provided to customers? NO
2) Service provided to the company? YES, employees worked for the company
3) Asset other than cash used (up)? NO

Salary expense or wages expense is reported on the income statement.

g. Advertising flyers were placed on potential customers' doors.

1) Goods or service provided to customers? NO
2) Service provided to the company? YES, advertising
3) Asset other than cash used (up)? NO

Advertising expense is reported on the income statement.

h. A new lawn was planted for a customer.

1) Goods or service provided to customers? YES, lawn service revenue
2) Service provided to the company? NO
3) Asset other than cash used (up)? NO

Lawn service revenue is reported on the income statement.

i. Supplies (grass squares) were used up.

1) Goods or service provided to customers? NO
2) Service provided to the company? NO
3) Asset other than cash used (up)? YES, supplies

Supplies expense is reported on the income statement.

j. An insurance company provided liability coverage for the business.

1) Goods or service provided to customers? NO
2) Service provided to the company? YES, insurance coverage
3) Asset other than cash used (up)? NO, assuming the cost was not prepaid

Insurance expense is reported on the income statement.

It is very important to notice that **when cash is received or paid is not considered** when preparing the income statement. The income statement does not report that cash was received or paid. The income statement reports economic events that happened <u>during the period</u> to earn income. This follows the **accrual basis of accounting.**

Generally accepted accounting principles require the use of <u>accrual basis accounting.</u>

The **accrual basis income statement** reports the following for a period of time:

Revenue is reported when <u>goods or services are provided</u> to customers.

- Expenses are reported when a <u>service is provided to the company</u> or an <u>asset is used</u> in order to generate revenue

_____

= Earnings for a period of time

Reporting economic transactions that occurred during the specific period of time, regardless of when cash is exchanged, reflects the earnings for a specific period of time.

The **cash basis income statement** reports the net change in cash for the period.

Revenues are reported when <u>cash is received</u> from customers.

- Expenses are reported when <u>cash is paid</u> for services or assets provided to the company.

_____

= Change in cash for a period of time

Net change in cash is **not** a proper reflection of the <u>earnings</u> of the business during the period because:

1) cash is not always received in the same period of time the services or goods are provided to customers.

2) cash is not always paid in the same period of time the service is received or assets are used to produce revenues.

<u>Earnings</u> for a particular period of time must be determined by comparing the value of goods and services provided to customers to the cost of providing those same goods and services during the **same** period of time.

 The cash basis of accounting is NOT acceptable under generally accepted accounting principles and is not used by accountants to report earnings. **Example 4-3** on the following page illustrates why reporting cash is NOT the same as reporting earnings.

45

Example 4-3 compares the cash basis to the accrual basis of accounting.

On January 1, 2012, Canterbury Publishing sold three year subscriptions of its quarterly publication, *Windy City Living*, to 2,500 subscribers. The full subscription price of $300 (12 issues at $25 per issue) for all three years was collected on January 2, 2012. Equipment with a total cost of $500,000 was purchased on January 2, 2012. The equipment is expected to be used for eight years. The cost of publishing and distributing the magazine is $60 annually per subscriber and is paid in cash as the cost is incurred.

For the Year Ended December 31, 2012

	Cash Basis:	**Accrual Basis:**
Sales:	$750,000 ($300 x 2,500)	$250,000 (1 year only; $100 x 2,500)
Costs:		
Publishing/distribution	$150,000 ($60 x 2,500)	$150,000 ($60 x 2,500)
Equipment	$500,000	$ 62,500 (1 year only;
Total Costs	$650,000	$212,500 $500,000 / 8 years)
Net:	$100,000	$ 37,500

The cash basis statement reports the amount of cash received and the amount of cash paid during the year 2012. Customers pay for all magazines in the first year. The cost of the equipment is all paid in the first year. The receipt and payment of cash does not occur in the same period the magazines are provided to customers or the equipment is used to produce the magazines. Publishing and distribution costs are paid for in the same year the services are provided to the company to produce the magazines. The company has $100,000 more cash at the end of the year.

The accrual basis statement reports the <u>earnings</u> from operating the business during 2012. Sales represent the value of magazines provided to customers during 2012 only. Publishing and distribution costs are for the services provided to the company to produce magazines during 2012 only. The expense for equipment is the estimated cost of using the equipment during 2012 only (one year out of eight total years the equipment is expected to be used.) Matching the revenues and expenses that happened during 2012 will result in earnings for the year 2012. The company <u>earned</u> $37,500 from operations during 2012.

Revenues must be collected and expenses must be paid. <u>When</u> the cash is collected or paid does not determine <u>when</u> the event is reported on the accrual basis income statement.

46

Example 4-3 continued

For the Year Ended December 31, 2013

	Cash Basis:	Accrual Basis:	
Sales:	$ 0	$250,000	(1 year)
Costs:			
Publishing/distribution	$150,000	$150,000	(1 year)
Equipment	$ 0	$ 62,500	(1 year)
Total Costs	$150,000	$212,500	
Net:	($150,000)	$ 37,500	

For the Year Ended December 31, 2014

	Cash Basis:	Accrual Basis:	
Sales:	$ 0	$250,000	(1 year)
Costs:			
Publishing/distribution	$150,000	$150,000	(1 year)
Equipment	$ 0	$ 62,500	(1 year)
Total Costs	$150,000	$212,500	
Net:	($150,000)	$ 37,500	

The cash basis statement reports no sales for 2013 and 2014 because all cash was collected in 2012. No cost of equipment is reported because the equipment was paid for in 2012. Publishing and distribution costs are incurred and paid in the same period. The net cash does not report the economic activities of the business during 2013 and 2014.

The accrual basis statement reports the value of magazines provided to customers and the costs associated with providing the magazines during 2013 and 2014. The earnings for each year are properly reported because expenses to generate revenue are reported in the same period the revenue is generated. The business has the same activities each year and it is reasonable that the business would earn the same amount each year from doing the same transactions.

The accrual basis statement reports the **earnings** during a period of time; not the net cash.

Businesses must keep track of cash; however, it is very misleading to measure the performance for a period of time using net cash. **The accrual basis of accounting is required by generally accepted accounting principles.**

5. More on the Income Statement

The value of goods and services provided to customers and the cost to provide to customers during a specific period of time is reported on the income statement. The income statement does not consider when cash was received or paid.

The accrual basis of accounting is required under generally accepted accounting principles because it best represents the results (earnings) of the economic events that occurred during the period.

The accrual basis income statement reports the following:

1) Revenues

Goods or services provided **to customers** during the period.

2) Expenses

Services provided **to the company** during the period.

Assets other than cash used (up) to provide goods or services to customers during the period.

3) Gains and Losses

The difference in the cash received from selling (or disposing of) an asset and the reported value of the asset sold.

The amount of revenues reported on the income statement is the value of the goods or services provided to customers during the period. The company is not always paid for the goods or services during the same period the goods or services are provided. The company must expect to receive cash at some point. Expenses occur when a service is provided to the company or an asset is used to provide goods or services to customers. Expenses are not always paid in the period they are incurred. All expenses are paid at some point.

Expenses occur when a service is provided to the company.

The common name of the expense is:	The service that was provided to the company is:
Utilities expense	Electricity, water, and other utilities
Salaries or Wage expense	Employees worked
Insurance expense	Coverage for liability, property damage, etc.
Rent expense	Use of an asset owned by another company
Advertising expense	Promoting the business to potential customers
Interest expense	The use of other's money

A company may pay for the service in the same period the service is received, or the payment may occur before (prepaid) or after (liability) the service is received. When cash is paid does not determine when the expense is reported on the income statement. The expense is reported for the period the service is provided to the company.

Expenses occur when items owned by the company are used (up) to provide goods or services to customers.

Assets that are used (up) to operate the business are supplies, prepaid expenses, inventory, property, plant, and equipment, and intangible assets. The cost of the asset is removed from the balance sheet and reported on the income statement as an expense when the asset is used. The name of the expense indicates which asset was used.

Some assets are used up completely and are no longer available to use, such as inventory, supplies, and prepaid assets. Some long-term assets are used and remain available for future use, such as property, plant, and equipment and intangibles. A long-term asset is reported on the balance sheet as long as it is still available for use.

Using Inventory

Inventory is purchased for the purpose of selling to customers. The expense, called **cost of goods sold**, is reported on the income statement when the inventory is provided to the customer. This is the same time period the revenue from the sale of goods is reported.

Using Supplies

Supplies are purchased to use to operate the day to day business. Supplies are reported as assets on the balance sheet until the supplies are used up. The expense of using the supplies, called **supplies expense**, is reported in the same time period the supplies are used to generate revenues.

50

Using Prepaid Expenses

Services paid for before the service is provided to the company is an asset called prepaid expense. The most common prepaid expenses are for insurance, rent and advertising. Insurance and rent are time based services. As time passes, the service is provided, the prepayment is no longer, and the asset is used up. **Insurance expense** or **rent expense** occurs when time passes and the cost is no longer prepaid. The cost of the asset is removed from the balance sheet and an expense is reported on the income statement.

The cost of advertising is often paid before the advertisement is provided. The cost is initially reported on the balance sheet as prepaid advertising. Prepaid advertising is removed from the balance sheet and **advertising expense** is reported on the income statement during the period advertising is provided.

Using Property, Plant, and Equipment

Property, plant, and equipment is reported on the balance sheet at cost when purchased. Each long-term asset, other than land, is assigned an estimated length of time in years the asset is expected to be used. A portion of the cost of the asset is expensed each year the asset is used. The expense related to using plant, and equipment is called **depreciation expense.** Land is not expensed because it never has to be replaced and is never used up.

Accountants estimate the annual expense of using an asset by spreading the **net cost** over the total estimated years the asset is expected to be used. Net cost is equal to historical cost less residual value. **Residual value** is the amount the asset is expected to be sold for when the company is finished using the asset.

The **straight-line method** will be used in this book to allocate expense to each year the plant and equipment is used. The formula for computing straight-line depreciation expense is as follows:

$$\frac{\text{Historical Cost} - \text{Residual Value}}{\text{Estimated Useful Life in Years}} = \text{Annual Depreciation Expense}$$

The straight-line method reports an equal amount of expense each year the asset is used.

Accountants use an account called **accumulated depreciation,** a negative "contra" asset account, to reduce property, plant, and equipment. The long-term asset must continue to be reported at historical cost. The accumulated depreciation account is used to reduce the asset and represents the cost of using the asset for <u>the total amount of time that has passed</u>. The two accounts (property, plant and equipment and accumulated depreciation) are presented together net on the balance sheet and the net amount represents the portion of the cost that has not yet been expensed. The "net cost" is often referred to as **book value**.

Example 5-1 illustrates how property, plant, and equipment and the cost of using property, plant, and equipment is reported on the financial statements.

A machine is purchased at a cost of $50,000. The machine is expected to be used for ten years and be sold for $10,000 at the end of ten years. The estimated expense for each year the machine is expected to be used is computed as follows:

$$\frac{\$50,000 - \$10,000}{10 \text{ years}} = \$4,000 \text{ expense each year for 10 years}$$

The balance sheet as of the end of the year and the income statement for the year will report the following for the first three years:

Balance Sheet:	End of Year 1	End of Year 2	End of Year 3
Machine (1)	$ 50,000	$50,000	$50,000
- Accumulated Depreciation (2)	($ 4,000)	($ 8,000)	($12,000)
= Property, Plant & Equipment, net (3)	$ 46,000	$42,000	$38,000

Income Statement:	Year 1	Year 2	Year 3
Depreciation Expense (4)	$4,000	$4,000	$4,000

(1) The cost of the machine does not change. It is always accounted for and reported at the historical cost of $50,000.

(2) Accumulated depreciation is used to reduce the machine for the estimated amount of cost that has been used to date. The amount is the total <u>cumulative</u> amount of depreciation expense for all the years the machine has been used to date. Accumulated depreciation increases each year the asset is used.

(3) Property, Plant & Equipment, **net** decreases each year the asset is used. The **net amount** is the cost that will be **expensed in future years.**

(4) The expense of using the machine is spread equally over each year the asset is used. The depreciation expense is the estimated cost of using the machine <u>for one year only</u>. The income statement reports the expense for one period of time only.

Very important: The balance sheet does not report the fair market value of long-term assets. Net is not intended to approximate fair market value and it does not represent how much the asset is worth. Net represents the amount that is expected to be expensed in the future. The net amount is reduced by the same amount that is reported on the income statement for the period.

Using Intangible Assets

The cost of using an intangible asset is determined similar to the cost of using property, plant, and equipment. The accountant estimates the total time in years the company is expected to benefit from using the asset. The cost of the asset is allocated to each year the asset is expected to be used. An expense is reported on the income statement each year the company receives benefit from exercising their exclusive right.

The intangible asset is always reported at historical cost. **Accumulation amortization** is a negative "contra" asset account that is used to show the reduction to the intangible asset each year the asset is used. The cost of using an intangible asset is called **amortization expense.** Amortization expense is computed using the straight-line method.

Example 5-2 illustrates how intangible assets and the cost of using intangible assets are reported on the financial statements.

The Company purchased a patent for $40,000. The patent is expected to be used to produce revenue for 10 years and then be obsolete by other patents. The estimated amortization expense for each year is computed using the straight-line method as follows:

$$\frac{\$40,000 - \$0}{10 \text{ years}} = \$4,000 \text{ estimated amortization expense each year}$$

The balance sheet as of the end of the year and the income statement for the year will report the following for the first three years:

Balance Sheet:	End of Year 1	End of Year 2	End of Year 3
Patent (1)	$40,000	$40,000	$40,000
- Accumulated Amortization (2)	($ 4,000)	($ 8,000)	($12,000)
Patent, net (3)	$36,000	$32,000	$28,000
Income Statement:	**Year 1**	**Year 2**	**Year 3**
Amortization Expense (4)	$4,000	$4,000	$4,000

(1) The cost of the patent does not change. The patent is always at historical cost of $40,000.

(2) Accumulated amortization (a contra asset) is used to reduce the patent for the estimated amount that has been used to date. The amount is the total <u>cumulative</u> amount of amortization expense for all the years the patents have been used. Accumulated amortization increases by the same amount of the expense each year an expense is reported on the income statement.

(3) Patent, **net** decreases each year the asset is used. The **net amount** is the cost that is expected to be **expensed in future years. Net does not represent fair market value.**

(4) The amortization expense is the estimated cost of using the patent <u>for one year only</u>.

All intangible assets with a definite time the company has the right to use the asset are used up as time passes. An expense is reported for using intangible assets that will eventually expire and have to be replaced. Goodwill is not expensed because it is not considered to be used up as time passes.

Depreciation expense and amortization expense is the cost of using long-term assets that are **owned** by the company. The cost of using assets that are **not owned** by the company is called **rent expense.**

The use of assets changes the accounting equation because the company has less total assets. Revenues increase assets because an asset is received from the customer in exchange for the goods or services. If the asset side of the accounting equation changes, something on the other side of the accounting equation must also change to keep the accounting equation in balance.

Revenue less expenses equals earnings. Earnings for each period are moved to retained earnings which is part of stockholders' equity. Revenues and expenses change the stockholders' equity part of the accounting equation.

Assets	=	Liabilities	+	Stockholders' Equity
- Asset used up	=			Expenses reduce earnings and retained earnings
+ Asset received in exchange	=			Revenue increases earnings and retained earnings

Expenses decrease stockholders' equity because expenses decrease earnings.
Revenue increase stockholders' equity because revenue increases earnings.

The accounting equation changes when a service is provided to the company. The company will either 1) pay for the service ahead of time and a prepaid is used up, 2) pay for the service during the period it is provided to the company, or 3) pay for the service in a future period.

	Assets	=	Liabilities	+	Stockholders' Equity
1)	- Asset used up	=			- Expenses reduce earnings and retained earnings
2)	- Asset used up	=			- Expenses reduce earnings and retained earnings
3)		=	+ More is owed		- Expenses reduce earnings and retained earnings

54

Two **common formats** are used for the income statement.

1) Companies that sell goods use a <u>multi-step</u> income statement.

A multi-step income statement is organized from top to bottom as follows:

1) Earnings from selling goods only (gross profit)

2) Expenses required to operate the primary day to day business of providing goods and services to customers (operating expenses.)

3) Items not related to the primary day to day business of providing goods and services to customers.

4) Earnings expected to continue in future years.
   (income from continuing operations.)

5) Items that are not expected to impact earnings in future years.
   (extraordinary items and discontinued operations)

It is common to report items that are greater than 10% of sales on a separate line item; however, this is not required by generally accepted accounting principles. Each company is allowed to determine the level of detail they believe is important for users to know.

Format of a Multi-step income statement:

```
    Sales
-   Cost of Goods Sold
=   Gross Profit
-   Operating Expenses:
        General and Administrative
        Selling and Marketing
        Research & Development
        Restructuring
=   Operating Income
+ -     Other Revenues and Expenses:
        Interest Income or Expense
        Rent Income
        Gains or Losses on Sale of Assets or Unusual Events
=   Income Before Taxes
    -   Income Tax Expense
=   Income from Continuing Operations
+ - Gain or Loss on Extraordinary Items
+ - Gain or Loss on Discontinued Operations
=       Net Income
```

The following line items and categories reported on the multi-step income statement are important to understand:

Sales consists of the value of goods (total price) provided to customers. Sales value is the amount the customer is expected to pay the company for the goods or services.

Cost of goods sold is the cost the company paid for the goods that were sold to customers. Cost is the amount paid to the supplier when goods are purchased ready to sell from another supplier. This occurs with retailers or distributors. Cost includes all material costs, labor costs, and costs to operate the manufacturing facility when the company manufactures goods.

Gross profit is the sales price less the cost to buy or manufacture the goods that were sold. This is the profit earned directly from selling inventory.

Operating expenses are directly related to primary day to day business operations. The primary business is what the company does to provide to customers. Operating expenses are often presented in the following summary categories:

1) Selling and Marketing: expenses related to acquiring new customers
   (advertising, shipping, sales people salaries, etc.)

2) General and Administrative: expenses related to operating the organization
   (accounting salaries, corporate office rent, business insurance, etc.)

3) Research & Development: expenses related to developing new products

4) Restructuring of Operations: expenses incurred to reduce future operating expenses
   (consolidating facilities, laying off employees, closing unprofitable stores, etc.)

Operating income is earnings from the primary day to day business that is expected to continue in the future.

Other revenues and expenses result from transactions that are **not** part of the primary day to day business of providing to customers. Examples of other revenues and expenses follow:

Interest expense:	the cost of borrowing money
Gains or losses:	the result of selling assets for more or less than net cost
Rent income:	earned from leasing excess space to others
Interest income:	earned from investing excess cash
Dividend income:	earned from investing excess cash

Unusual gains and losses that are may occur in future periods are reported as other. This includes losses from theft or fire or natural disasters common to the geographical area.

Other revenues and expenses are also called non-operating revenues and expenses.

Income tax expense is the amount that must be paid to the government based on a percentage of income before tax. The percentage is set by the internal revenue service (IRS.) The amount of income tax expense that is reported for a company with income before tax of $100,000 when the IRS rate is 35% is computed as follows:

Income Before Tax	$100,000
x IRS %	35%
= Income Tax Expense	$ 35,000

Income tax is reported separately because management has very little control over the amount.

Income from continuing operations is the earnings related to activity that is expected to continue to occur in future periods. This is often used to project future earnings.

Gain or loss on discontinued operations results from selling or disposing of a significant separate part of the business. This includes eliminating or selling significant product lines or moving out of a distinct geographic area. A discontinued operation occurs when a company is no longer be involved in operating any portion of that segment of the business.

Restructuring, which is not discontinued operations, occurs when the company continues to operate that segment of the business and implements significant changes to improve future earnings.

Extraordinary items are unusual and infrequent. A gain or loss from an extraordinary item is generally not expected to ever happen again. Items that are only unusual or only infrequent are reported as other revenue or expense. An occurrence must be both unusual and infrequent to be reported as an extraordinary item. An example of an extraordinary item is a flood in a California desert or a foreign government seizing assets in a foreign country.

Discontinued operations and extraordinary items are included in income under IRS rules. The results are taxable; however, gains and losses are reported net of the tax impact on the income statement because these items are reported below the income tax expense line item.

Net income is the total earnings from operating the business during the period.

The order of the income statement provides the user with the results of the various types of activities of the company. It is important to consider separately the gross profit from selling products, the cost of providing to customers, items not related to servicing customers and items not expected to occur in the future when projecting future earnings.

Example 5-3 presents the income statement for Intel Corporation. Intel Corporation manufactures and sells computer hardware.

Gross margin reflects earnings from selling hardware only. Operating expenses represent the cost of running the day to day business. Research and development is a significant expense and is reported separately. Restructuring expense is the cost of reorganizing the operations of the business in order to earn more income in the future. Amortization is the cost of using long-term intangible assets. Operating income is the earnings from the primary day to day business of selling goods to customers.

Below operating income are gains and losses from selling investments and other amounts earned. These items are not part of the primary purpose of selling goods to customers. Provision for taxes is the amount that must be paid to the government for earnings. Provision is another word for expense. Net income is the total earnings for the year. Earnings per share is discussed at the end of this chapter.

INTEL CORPORATION
CONSOLIDATED STATEMENTS OF INCOME

Three Years Ended December 25, 2010
(In Millions, Except Per Share Amounts)

	2010	2009	2008
Net revenue	$43,623	$35,127	$37,586
Cost of sales	15,132	15,566	16,742
Gross margin	28,491	19,561	20,844
Research and development	6,576	5,653	5,722
Marketing, general and administrative	6,309	7,931	5,452
Restructuring and asset impairment charges	—	231	710
Amortization of acquisition-related intangibles	18	35	6
Operating expenses	12,903	13,850	11,890
Operating income	15,588	5,711	8,954
Gains (losses) on equity method investments, net	117	(147)	(1,380)
Gains (losses) on other equity investments, net	231	(23)	(376)
Interest and other, net	109	163	488
Income before taxes	16,045	5,704	7,686
Provision for taxes	4,581	1,335	2,394
Net income	$11,464	$ 4,369	$ 5,292
Basic earnings per common share	$ 2.06	$ 0.79	$ 0.93
Diluted earnings per common share	$ 2.01	$ 0.77	$ 0.92

Each company decides which line items are important enough to list separately and which items are combined with other items. It is unusual for a company to present a separate line for items with small dollars (such as amortization of acquisition related intangibles shown above.) The goal of the company should be to provide the most useful information for decision making. Sorting the information by purpose and presenting three years of information allows the user to compare one year to another and project future years using prior year trends.

2) Service companies that do not sell goods use a <u>single step</u> income statement.

A single step income statement subtotals all types of revenue and all types of operating expenses. Total revenue less total operating expenses nets to operating income. Items below operating income are reported in the same format as the multi-step income statement.

Format of the Single Step Income Statement:

```
   Software Revenue
 + Service Revenue
     = Total Revenue

 - General and Administrative
 - Selling and Marketing
 - Research & Development
 - Restructuring
       Total Operating Expenses

 = Operating Income
 + - Other Revenues and Expenses:
       Interest Income or Expense
       Rent Income
       Gains or losses on sales of assets or unusual events
 = Income Before Tax
  - Income Tax Expense
 = Income from Continuing Operations
 + - Gain or Loss on Extraordinary Items
 + - Gain or Loss on Discontinued Operations
 =        Net Income
```

Notice the following:

1) The single step income statement does not report gross profit.
   A company that uses this statement does not primarily sell goods.

2) The types of operating expenses are the same for both the multi-step and the single step income statement.

3) The format for all items presented below operating income is the same for both the multi-step and the single step income statement.

Important: The only difference in the multi-step income statement and the single step income statement is cost of goods sold and gross profit is not reported on the single step.

Example 5-4 presents a single step income statement for Chipotle Mexican Grill, Inc. (CMG.) This company operates restaurants. Cost of goods sold and gross profit is not reported. The company views all expenses as costs of providing the services of food and atmosphere. All costs related to the company's primary business of operating restaurants are subtracted from revenues to arrive at income from operations. Notice that CMG considers the loss on disposal of assets as an operating expense because it is a normal cost of operating restaurants. Items reported below income from operations are not related to the day to day business of serving customers.

CHIPOTLE MEXICAN GRILL, INC.
CONSOLIDATED STATEMENT OF INCOME
(in thousands, except per share data)

| | Years ended December 31 | | |
	2010	2009	2008
Revenue	$ 1,835,922	$ 1,518,417	$ 1,331,968
Restaurant operating costs (exclusive of depreciation and amortization shown separately below):			
Food, beverage and packaging	561,107	466,027	431,947
Labor	453,573	385,072	351,005
Occupancy	128,933	114,218	98,071
Other operating costs	202,904	174,581	164,018
General and administrative expenses	118,590	99,149	89,155
Depreciation and amortization	68,921	61,308	52,770
Pre-opening costs	7,767	8,401	11,624
Loss on disposal of assets	6,296	5,956	9,339
Total operating expenses	1,548,091	1,314,712	1,207,929
Income from operations	**287,831**	**203,705**	**124,039**
Interest and other income	1,499	925	3,469
Interest and other expense	(269)	(405)	(302)
Income before income taxes	289,061	204,225	127,206
Provision for income taxes	(110,080)	(77,380)	(49,004)
Net income	**$ 178,981**	**$ 126,845**	**$ 78,202**
Earnings per share			
Basic	$ 5.73	$ 3.99	$ 2.39
Diluted	$ 5.64	$ 3.95	$ 2.36
Weighted average common shares outstanding			
Basic	31,234	31,766	32,766
Diluted	31,735	32,102	33,146

Each company is allowed to determine which method of presentation provides the most useful information. The single step is used primarily by service companies and the multi-step is used primarily by companies that sell goods. Companies that provide a significant amount of goods and a significant amount of services often use a mixture of the two formats.

Example 5-5 presents the income statement for General Electric Company. General Electric manufactures and sells products and also provides services. The company presents a mixture of a multi-step and single step income statement.

Statement of Earnings

For the years ended December 31 (In millions; per-share amounts in dollars)		2011		2010		2009
General Electric Company and consolidated affiliates						
Revenues						
Sales of goods	$	66,875	$	60,812	$	65,067
Sales of services		27,648		39,625		38,710
Other income		5,063		1,151		1,006
GECS revenues from services		47,714		48,005		49,655
Total revenues		147,300		149,593		154,438
Costs and expenses						
Cost of goods sold		51,455		46,005		50,580
Cost of services sold		16,823		25,708		25,341
Interest and other financial charges		14,545		15,553		17,697
Investment contracts, insurance losses and insurance annuity benefits		2,912		3,012		3,017
Provision for losses on financing receivables		4,083		7,176		10,585
Other costs and expenses		37,384		38,054		37,354
Total costs and expenses		127,202		135,508		144,574
Earnings (loss) from continuing operations before income taxes		20,098		14,085		9,864
Benefit (provision) for income taxes		(5,732)		(1,033)		1,142
Earnings from continuing operations		14,366		13,052		11,006
Earnings (loss) from discontinued operations, net of taxes		77		(873)		219
Net earnings		14,443		12,179		11,225

Earnings per Share

Companies are required to report earnings per share (EPS) on the income statement. Earnings per share represent earnings of one share of common stock, and is computed as follows:

$$\frac{\text{Net Income} - \text{Preferred Dividends}}{\text{Average number of Common Shares Outstanding}} = \text{Earnings per Share}$$

Earnings per share is related to common shares. Dividends paid to preferred stockholders are subtracted from net income because this part of earnings is not available to common stockholders. Earnings per share is presented two ways: basic and diluted.

Basic EPS uses the number of common shares <u>currently</u> outstanding. Outstanding means the shares are owned by stockholders outside the company.

Diluted EPS uses the number of common shares that <u>could be outstanding</u> given all the financial instruments currently owned that could be exchanged for common shares, were exchanged for common shares.

Example 5-6 illustrates the difference in Basic EPS and Diluted EPS.

Company actual weighted average number of shares:	100,000	Used in Basic EPS
Stock Options that can be converted into common stock in the future	10,000	
Debt that could be repaid with the issuance of common stock rather than paying cash to the lender	<u>15,000</u>	
Total common stock shares that could be outstanding	125,000	Used in Diluted EPS

Diluted EPS is reported to show investors how low earnings per share could be given additional common shares related to current commitments are issued in the future.

Financial instruments that can be exchanged for common shares are stock options and warrants to purchase the stock at a set price, debt convertible into common stock, and preferred stock convertible into common stock. Diluted EPS is the "worst case scenario" of how low EPS could go given current net income remains the same.

Earnings per share is often used by investors to determine the market value of one share of common stock. An investor may multiply earnings per share by an expected growth percentage to determine the estimated fair market value (price) for one share.

A higher EPS and a higher rate of growth, generally leads to a higher fair market value for one share of stock.

Example 5-7 demonstrates how the earnings per share of Chipotle Mexican Grill, Inc (CMG) may be used to estimate the fair market value (FMV) of one share of common stock of CMG.

The percentage growth rate for CMG follows:

Year	Earnings per Share	Annual EPS Growth
2008	$ 2.39	
2009	$ 3.99	67% *
2010	$ 5.73	44% **
2011	$ 6.80 estimated	19%
2012	$ 8.89 estimated	31%
2013	$11.11 estimated	24%

   * $3.99 - $2.39 = $1.60 / $2.39 = 67%
 ** $5.73 - $3.99 = $1.74 / $3.99 = 44%

Given investors expect the company to grow earnings per share at an average of 25% for several years in the future, the estimated fair market value would be computed as follows:

CMG 2010 EPS	$5.73	(see example 5-4)
x Expected growth percentage	25	
= Estimated FMV of a share of stock:	$143	

An investor who expects CMG to grow at 40% annually for several years into the future would estimate the current fair market value of one share of stock as follows:

CMG 2010 EPS	$5.73
x Expected growth percentage	40
= Estimated FMV of a share of stock:	$229

The actual fair market value of one share of common stock was $212 on December 31, 2010. An investor who expects CMG to grow at 25% annually for several years into the future may believe stock at a price of $212 to be overvalued and may lose value in the future. Investors who expect the company to grow earnings per share at approximately 40% in future years may think the stock is approximately fairly valued.

Actual earnings per share for the year ended December 31, 2011 was $6.80 and the fair market value of one share of CMG appreciated to $338. Earnings per share is estimated to be $11.11 for the year ended 2013. Given EPS of $11.11, the expected fair value could be as follows:

CMG 2010 EPS	$11.11
x Expected growth percentage	30
= Estimated FMV of a share of stock:	$ 333

Investors willing to pay $338 per share are most likely expecting 30% growth for an extended period of years.

Earnings per share can play a significant part in determining the fair market value of one share.

6. Revenues and Expenses Change the Balance Sheet

Revenues and expenses are reported on the income statement in the period they are <u>earned</u> or <u>incurred</u>, NOT when cash is paid or received. When cash is paid or received does not affect the income statement. This chapter will discuss how the balance sheet reports <u>when</u> the cash exchange occurred or is expected to occur.

The balance sheet can change without anything being reported on the income statement (see chapter 3.) Cash exchanges related to current period revenue or expenses may occur in the previous period, in the same period, or in a future period. A change to the income statement will always change an item on the balance sheet.

An expense occurs when an asset is used to provide goods or services to operate the business. Cash paid for the asset often occurs in a different period than the asset is used.

Think of it like this for <u>revenues</u>:

1) Goods and services are provided to the customer and the revenue is earned and reported on the income statement even if the customer does not pay the company in the same time period the goods or service is provided to the customer.

2) Along with the revenue comes more cash, **or** more accounts receivable, **or** less unearned revenue.

> **2 Things:**   1st the **revenue,** and
>
>   2nd a **balance sheet account** changes

The most common balance sheet accounts that change when the cash exchange occurs in a different period than the revenues is reported on the income statement are **unearned revenue** and various types of **receivables**.

<u>**Unearned Revenue (also called deferred revenue)**</u> is used when cash was received by the company in a period **<u>before</u>** the goods or services were provided to the customer. The company owes the customer until the goods or services are provided. Unearned revenue is a liability. Unearned revenue leaves the balance sheet and is reported as revenue on the income statement in the period goods or services are provided to the customer who previously paid. Examples of unearned revenues are as follows:
   1) A customer pays before the goods are shipped in order to guarantee that the goods will be shipped on a future date.
   2) A customer pays for a 3 year service contract at the beginning of the first year.
   3) Gift cards paid for before the gift card is used to purchase goods.

A **receivable** is reported on the balance sheet when the company expects to be paid in a **period after** goods or services are provided.   A receivable is an amount owed to the company. Cash is normally expected to be received by the company in 30 days.
The most common types of receivable are as follows:

1) Accounts Receivable: customers owe the company for goods or services.
2) Credit Card Receivable: customers paid for goods or services with a credit card and the bank issuing the credit card owes the company.
3) Interest Receivable: the company is owed for interest.
4) Rent Receivable: the company is owed for the use of the company's excess space.
5) Dividend Receivable: the company is owed money related to their investments.

Think of it like this for expenses:

1) The company is provided a service and the expense is reported on the income statement when the service is received by the company even if the company does not pay in the same period the company receives the service.

2) Along with the expense comes less prepaid expense, **or** less cash, **or** more payable.

> **2 Things:**   1st the **expense,** and
>
>   2nd a **balance sheet account** changes

The common balance sheet accounts used to report <u>when</u> the cash exchange occurs for expenses are **prepaid expenses** and various types of **current liabilities.**

Prepaid expense is used when cash is paid in a period **before** the service is provided to the company. This is normally related to insurance, rent, or advertising. The prepaid expense becomes an expense when the service is provided. This was discussed in chapter 2.

Many different current liability account names are used to indicate an amount is owed by the company for services received. The most common items reported on the balance sheet are as follows:

Accounts payable is used when cash is paid in a period **after** receiving services. Accounts payable is <u>owed</u> to suppliers. Suppliers provide to the company repeatedly and send the company a monthly invoice. The company typically pays 30 days after receiving a monthly invoice. Items purchased on credit card are generally reported as accounts payable.

"_____" **payable** is used when cash is paid in a period **after** the company receives a specific service and the amount is large enough to report separately on the balance sheet. The name of the payable describes the service received. Common names used are salaries payable, wages payable, rent payable, interest payable, and taxes payable. These types of expense are normally not invoiced. If an item is not large enough to be reported separately, it is included in accrued expenses. Generally an amount greater than 10% of total current liabilities is reported with a separate line item.

Accrued expenses (also called accrued liabilities) is used when cash is paid in a period **after** services are received by the company. Accrued expenses or accrued liabilities generally consist of liabilities owed in the course of business that are not repeat purchases. Accrued means "not yet paid."

There is effectively no difference between accounts payable and accrued liabilities; both accounts represent amounts owed for services provided to the company. Accounts payable consists of routine invoices that are sent to the company and processed daily by the accounting department, such as utilities, maintenance, cleaning services. Accrued liabilities consist of items that are not typically invoiced, such as rent or employee bonuses.

Examples 6-1 and 6-2 on the following pages provide a closer look at how the balance sheet reports **when** cash is exchanged for revenues and expenses.

Revenue: **Example 6-1** The Company provided services valued at $2,000 to a customer.

If <u>cash</u> is received <u>before</u> the services are provided, the financial statements report the following:

Balance Sheet		Income Statement
Asset:	Liability:	
Cash +2,000	Unearned Revenue + 2,000	Nothing

Revenue will be earned and reported in a future period when the services are provided to the customer. The unearned revenue will be removed from the balance sheet and revenue will be reported on the income statement in a future period when the service is provided.

If <u>cash</u> is received in the <u>same period</u> the services are provided, the financial statements report the following:

Balance Sheet		Income Statement
Asset:	Liability:	
Cash +2,000	Nothing	Revenues + 2,000

Receiving the cash is not the reason revenue is reported on the income statement. Revenue is reported because the services were provided to customers.

If <u>cash</u> is received <u>after</u> the services are provided, the financial statements will report the following:

Balance Sheet		Income Statement
Asset:	Liability:	
Accounts Receivable + 2,000	Nothing	Revenues + 2,000

Revenue is reported in the period it is earned. The company has an accounts receivable until cash is collected in a future period. Revenue will not be reported again when cash is collected from the customer.

Expense: **Example 6-2** The Company received advertising services at a cost of $2,000.

If cash is paid before the service is provided to the company, the financial statements will report the following:

Balance Sheet		Income Statement
Asset:	Liability:	
Cash – 2,000	Nothing	Nothing
Prepaid Expense + 2,000		

    In the future, when the advertisement is run, the prepaid expense will be removed from the balance sheet and reported on the income statement as an expense. The expense is reported when the service is provided to the company.

If cash is paid in the same period the service is provided to the company, the financial statements will report the following:

Balance Sheet		Income Statement
Asset:	Liability:	
Cash -2,000	Nothing	Expense + 2,000

    The expense is reported in the period the service is provided to the company. The cash payment is not the reason the expense is reported on the income statement. The expense is reported on the income statement because the service was provided to the company

If cash is paid after the period the service is provided to the company, the financial statements will report the following:

Balance Sheet		Income Statement
Asset:	Liability:	
Nothing	Advertising Payable +2,000 (or accrued liabilities)	Expense + 2,000

    The expense is reported in the period the service is provided to the company. Advertising payable (or accrued liabilities) will be removed from the balance sheet and cash will be lower in the future when the liability is paid. The expense will not be reported again when the liability is paid.

An expense occurs when an <u>asset is used</u> to provide goods or services to customers.

A company purchases assets specifically to be used to provide goods and services to customers. An asset becomes an expense on the income statement when it is used to do business. All assets are expected to be exchanged for cash or to be used in the course of doing business. Assets not intended to be exchanged for cash will become expenses in a future period.

<u>Assets</u> that are commonly <u>used</u> and the associated <u>expense</u> that is reported on the income statement when the assets are used are as follows:

<u>Asset</u>   become an   <u>Expense</u>

Time passes and a prepaid expense is used up and is no longer prepaid.

Prepaid Rent Expense	*Rent Expense*
Prepaid Insurance Expense	*Insurance Expense*
Prepaid Advertising Expense	*Advertising Expense*

Supplies are used up and the company no longer has the supplies.

Supplies	*Supplies Expense*

Inventory is provided to customers and is no longer owned by the company.

Inventory	*Cost of Goods Sold*

The cost of a long-term asset is spread over the total time the asset is expected to be used to produce revenue.

Property, Plant, and Equipment	*Depreciation Expense*
Intangible Assets	*Amortization Expense*

Accounts receivable is not expected to be collected.

Accounts Receivable	*Bad Debt Expense*

Many companies provide goods to customers on account. The following four things change on the financial statements when goods are provided to customers:

1) Revenue (sales) occurs when the goods are provided to the customer.
2) The customer pays the company now (cash) or agrees to pay the company in a future period (accounts receivable or credit card receivable.)
3) Inventory is provided to the customer (less inventory.)
4) The cost of the inventory used up is an expense called cost of goods sold.

Example 6-3 illustrates how providing goods to customers is reported on the financial statements. Tick Tock, Inc. sold clocks that cost a total of $50,000 for a total sales price of $72,000, on account. The customers are expected to pay Tick Tock, Inc. in approximately 30 days. The balance sheet and the income statement will report the following:

Balance Sheet: Income Statement:

         Assets: Sales $72,000
                               - Cost of Goods Sold   ($50,000)

Accounts Receivable $72,000 more
Inventory   ($50,000) less   = Gross Profit $22,000

Earnings and total assets increase $22,000.

A common way to sell goods to customers is through the use of gift cards. Essentially, one customer pays for another customer to purchase goods in the future. The company receives the cash when the gift card is purchased. Revenue is not recorded until a customer uses the gift card to purchase goods or if not used, during the period the gift card expires.

Cash received for the sale of the gift card is initially reported as unearned revenue. The company has a liability to honor the gift card and provide goods to a customer in the future. Revenue is reported when the goods are provided to the customer.

The initial sale of a $50 gift card is reported on the balance sheet only as follows:

Assets: Liability:

Cash $50   Unearned Revenue $50

The use of the $50 gift card to purchase goods for a price of $50 that cost the company $30 changes the balance sheet and income statement as follows:

Balance Sheet: Income Statement:

Assets: Liability: Sales Revenue $50
                                          - Cost of goods sold   ($30)
Cash   no change   Unearned Revenue   ($50)   = Gross Profit $20
Inventory ($30)   (moves to income statement)

71

This statement shows the common accounts reported on the balance sheet in order of liquidity; sorted by assets, liabilities, and stockholders' equity. Accounts that indicate cash is received or paid in a different period than the revenue or expense is reported on the income statement are shown in italics.

Assets:

Cash
Accounts Receivable
Inventory
Supplies
Prepaid Expenses
"_____" Receivables
Notes or Financing Receivable
Short-term Investments
    Total Current Assets

Long-term Investments
L/T Notes or Financing Receivable

Property/Plant/Equipment (P/P/E):
  Land
  Building
  Furniture and Fixtures
  Equipment
  Vehicles
    Less Accumulated Depreciation
    Net P/P/E

Intangible Assets
  Goodwill
  Patents, net
  Copyrights, net
  Trademarks, net
    Total Intangible Assets

Other Long-term Assets

Total Assets

Liabilities:

Accounts Payable
Accrued Expenses or Accrued Liabilities
Unearned or Deferred Revenues (ST)
"_____" Payable (various payables)
Income Taxes Payable
Short-term Notes Payable
Current Maturities of Long-term Debt
    Total Current Liabilities

Unearned or Deferred Revenue (LT)
Long-term Debt
Bonds Payable

    Total Liabilities

Stockholders' Equity:

Common Stock
Additional Paid in Capital
Retained Earnings
Treasury Stock
Other Comprehensive Income
    Total Stockholder's Equity

=   **Total Liabilities & Stockholder's Equity**

Example 6-4 presents the balance sheet of Microsoft, Inc. You will notice that it follows the same format and uses common account names. Account names not discussed in this book are replaced with XXXXXXXX.

Example 6-4:

Microsoft, Inc.   BALANCE SHEETS

(In millions)

June 30,		2011		2010
Assets				
Current assets:				
Cash and cash equivalents	$	9,610	$	5,505
Short-term investments		43,162		31,283
Total cash, cash equivalents, and short-term investments		52,772		36,788
Accounts receivable, net of allowance for doubtful accounts of $333 and $375		14,987		13,014
Inventories		1,372		740
XXXXXXXXXXXXXXXXXXX		2,467		2,184
Other		3,320		2,950
Total current assets		74,918		55,676
Property and equipment, net of accumulated depreciation of $9,829 and $8,629		8,162		7,630
Equity and other investments		10,865		7,754
Goodwill		12,581		12,394
Intangible assets, net		744		1,158
Other long-term assets		1,434		1,501
Total assets	$	108,704	$	86,113
Liabilities and stockholders' equity				
Current liabilities:				
Accounts payable	$	4,197	$	4,025
Short-term debt		0		1,000
Accrued compensation		3,575		3,283
Income taxes		580		1,074
Short-term unearned revenue		15,722		13,652
XXXXXXXXXXXXXXXX		1,208		182
Other		3,492		2,931
Total current liabilities		28,774		26,147
Long-term debt		11,921		4,939
Long-term unearned revenue		1,398		1,178
XXXXXXXXXXXXXXXXXX		1,456		229
Other long-term liabilities		8,072		7,445
Total liabilities		51,621		39,938

Example 6-4 continued

Stockholders' equity:

Common stock and paid-in capital – shares authorized 24,000; outstanding **8,376** and 8,668	**63,415**	62,856
Retained deficit, including accumulated other comprehensive income of **$1,863** and $1,055	**(6,332)**	(16,681)
Total stockholders' equity	**57,083**	46,175
Total liabilities and stockholders' equity $	**108,704** $	86,113

Microsoft, Inc. is a manufacturer and seller of software and services. The accounts on its balance sheet report the company's financial position on June 30, 2011 and 2010. The balance sheet reports the following about the financial position of Microsoft, Inc.:

1) Microsoft, Inc. has almost $53 billion in cash and short-term investments that can be easily converted into cash.

2) Microsoft, Inc. expects to collect almost $15 billion from customers in the near future. Approximately $333 million owed by customers is not expected to be received.

3) Inventories represent a very minimal amount of total assets. The cost of producing software is not significant.

4) Microsoft, Inc. uses property and equipment to operate its business. The net cost of property and equipment that has not yet been expensed is approximately $8.2 billion. The total cost of using the property and equipment for all periods to date is approximately $9.8 billion. The fair market value of property and equipment is NOT reported on the balance sheet.

5) Microsoft, Inc. has invested over $10.8 billion in other companies it intends to hold for more than one year.

6) The increase in goodwill indicates Microsoft, Inc. purchased other companies during 2011. The total amount that has been paid for the companies over and above the net assets purchased is approximately $12.5 billion cumulative to date.

7) Microsoft, Inc. has $744 million of non physical assets used long term to generate revenues. The footnotes provide details of the types of intangible assets the company owns (patents, trademarks, copyrights, etc.) The amount is the net cost not yet expensed and does not represent fair market value.

8) The company owes suppliers approximately $4.2 billion (accounts payable) and owes approximately $3.6 billion related to employees (accrued compensation.)
Example 6-4 continued

9) Microsoft, Inc. repaid or refinanced short-term debt of $1 billion during 2011.

10) Customers have paid Microsoft, Inc. $15.7 billion for goods and services that are expected to be provided within the next year. Customers have paid $1.4 billion for goods and services that are expected to be provided after one year. (Unearned Revenue)

11) Microsoft, Inc. owes almost $12 billion for borrowings that are expected to be repaid in after one year. The borrowings could be from banks, financial institutions, or investors. A specific account name that specifically identifies who funds were borrowed from is not used. Additional details are provided in the footnotes.

12) The balance sheet reports other long-term liabilities of approximately $8.1 billion. The footnotes report that other long-term liabilities consist of $7.4 billion of tax related liabilities and $0.7 billion in liabilities for legal contingencies and other.

13) The $63.4 billion of common stock and paid in capital represents amounts received from investors for ownership in the company to date.

14) The retained deficit includes the total earnings of the company since beginning operations less amounts paid to stockholders, less amounts that have not yet been reported on the income statement (other comprehensive income), less treasury stock owned by Microsoft. The footnotes report significant purchases of treasury stock are the cause of the negative retained deficit. Microsoft has reported positive earnings for each year the company has been in business. Most companies show each account and amount separately.

Recording Transactions that Change the Balance Sheet and the Income Statement

Accountants record every transaction of the business in a way that is easy to summarize the net results. The net results are then reported on the balance sheet and the income statement.

The following five questions are used to determine what will be reported on the balance sheet and the income statement when a transaction occurs.

1) Were goods or services provided to customers?   revenue
    (If yes, was cash or a receivable exchanged? see 4.)
2) Was a service provided to the company?   expense
    (If yes, was cash paid or is there a liability? see 4. or 5.)
3) Was an asset other than cash used (up) during the period?   expense
4) Does the company have more or less?   asset
5) Does the company owe more or less?   liability

After answering the first two questions, determine if cash was received or paid this period. If cash was received or paid in a different period, an account other than cash is used: prepaid, receivable, unearned, or payable.

Example 6 -5 gives several transactions and illustrates how answering the five questions is used to determine what is reported on the balance sheet and income statement. The transactions below occurred at Pillow Soft, Inc. during **February,** the second month of business.

1. Employees worked and earned \$15,000. Employees are paid on the 2nd day of the following month.

A service was provided to the company. This is an expense related to employees called salary expense.

The fact that the employees were not paid until next month does not matter to the income statement. The expense is reported because the service was provided to the company. The balance sheet will report a liability until the 2nd of next month when the employees are paid cash.

1) Were goods and services provided to customers? **No**
2) Was a service provided to the company? **Yes, salaries expense; \$15,000**
3) Was an asset other than cash used up during the period? **No**
4) Does the company have more or less? **No, cash was not paid**
5) Does the company owe more or less? **Yes, salaries payable; \$15,000**

2. An advertising company was paid $2,400 for sending marketing brochures to potential customers in the current month.

A service was provided to the company. This is an expense related to advertising called advertising expense.

The expense is reported in the current month because this is when the service was provided. The fact that cash was paid does not make it an expense. The fact that the service was provided is what makes the transaction an expense.

1) Were goods and services provided to customers? **No**
2) Was a service provided to the company? **Yes, advertising expense; $2,400**
3) Was an asset other than cash used up during the period? **No**
4) Does the company have more or less? **Less, cash was paid; $2,400**
5) Does the company owe more or less? **No**

3. The company used rented warehouse and office facilities. The company paid $6,000 for the three months rent at the end of January.

Prepaid rent is an asset of the company because it was paid ahead of time.
The expense occurs in the time period the service is provided to the company.
One month of rent expense for $2,000 will be reported.
     ($6,000 / 3 months = $2,000 expense for one month)

1) Were goods and services provided to customers? **No**
2) Was a service provided to the company? **Yes, rent expense; $2,000**
3) Was an asset other than cash used up during the period? **Yes, prepaid rent; $2,000**
4) Does the company have more or less? **Yes, less prepaid rent; $2,000 (same as 3)**
5) Does the company owe more or less? **No**

4. The company was provided insurance coverage during the month. The company paid $12,000 for six months coverage at the end of January.

Prepaid insurance is an asset of the company because it was paid for ahead of time.
The expense occurs in the month the service is provided to the company.
 One month of expense for $2,000 is reported.
     ($12,000 / 6 months = $2,000 expense for one month)

1) Were goods and services provided to customers? **No**
2) Was a service provided to the company? **Yes, insurance expense; $2,000**
3) Was an asset other than cash used up during the period? **Yes,**
                                                   prepaid insurance; $2,000
4) Does the company have more or less? **Yes, less prepaid; $2,000 (same as 3.)**
5) Does the company owe more or less? **No**

5. Customers were provided pillows for a price of $62,000. The cost of the pillows provided to customers was $28,000. The customers are expected to pay in 30 days.

Goods were provided to customers during the month. This is sales revenue.
The company has accounts receivable until the cash is collected from the customers

The inventory provided to customers is an asset that was used up, an expense.
The expense of using inventory is called cost of goods sold.

1) Were goods and services provided to customers? **Yes, Sales; $62,000**
2) Was a service was provided to the company? **No**
3) Was an asset other than cash used up during the period? **Yes,**
   Cost of Goods Sold; $28,000
4) Does the company have more or less? **Less Inventory; $28,000**
   More Accounts Receivable; $62,000
5) Does the company owe more or less? **No**

6. The company received the utility bill for February in the amount of $275 (not paid.)

A service was provided to the company on account that has not been paid.

The expense is reported in the current month, which is when the service is provided.

1) Were goods and services provided to customers? **No**
2) Was a service provided to the company? **Yes, utilities expense; $275**
3) Was an asset other than cash used up during the period? **No**
4) Does the company have more or less? **Nothing**
5) Does the company owe more or less? **Yes, accounts payable; $275**

7. The company used property, plant, and equipment during the February.

The balance sheet reports a cost of:	/	estimated useful life	= cost per month
Warehouse equipment	$50,000 /	7 years = 84 months	$ 595
Office Furniture	$15,000 /	10 years = 120 months	$ 125
Computer Equipment	$18,000 /	3 years = 36 months	$ 500
			$ 1,220

Using an asset to produce revenues is an expense. The use of long-term assets
 is called depreciation expense.

A total depreciation expense of $1,220 will be reported on the income statement
 for the use of the long-term assets for one month. The assets will continue
 to be reported on the balance sheet at the original cost.

78

Accumulated depreciation will be used to show the assets have been used. The amount of accumulated depreciation that will be reported on the balance sheet is also $1,220 because this is the first month the assets have been used.

1) Were goods and services provided to customers? **No**
2) Was a service provided to the company? **No**
3) Was an asset other than cash used up during the period? **Yes,**
   Depreciation Expense; $1,220
4) Does the company have more or less? **Less time to use the assets**
   Reported as negative accumulated depreciation; $1,220
5) Does the company owe more or less? **No**

8. Office supplies that cost $110 were used during February.

Using an asset to produce revenues is an expense. The amount of office supplies reported on the balance sheet will be $110 less and an expense is reported on the income statement.

1) Were goods and services provided to customers? **No**
2) Was a service provided to the company? **No**
3) Was an asset other than cash used up during the period? **Yes,**
   Office Supplies expense; $110
4) Does the company have more or less? **Less office supplies; $110**
5) Does the company owe more or less? **No**

It is the accountant's responsibility to record all transactions, summarize all transactions that occurred during the period, and report the financial position and results of operations on the financial statements. The spreadsheet on the next page is used to record and summarize transactions that occurred during February.

Balance sheet accounts are cumulative and do not start over each period. The beginning balance for balance sheet accounts is the ending balance from the previous period. See page 38 for the January 31st account balances for Pillow Soft, Inc.

Income statement accounts are for the current period only and must start at zero each period. Prior month income statement amounts were moved to retained earnings at the end of the previous month.

	Cash	Prepaid Insurance	Accounts Receivable	Inventory	Prepaid Rent	Office Supplies
Begin	$124,000	$12,000		$60,000	$6,000	$300
2)	($ 2,400)					
3)					($2,000)	
4)		($2,000)				
5)			$62,000	($28,000)		
8)						($110)
TOTAL	$121,600	$10,000	$62,000	$32,000	$4,000	$190

	Warehouse Equipment	Office Furniture	Computer Equipment	Accumulated Depreciation
Begin	$50,000	$15,000	$18,000	
7)				($1,220)
TOTAL	$50,000	$15,000	$18,000	($1,220)

	Accounts Payable	Salary Payable	Notes Payable	Common Stock	Office Supplies Expense	Rent Expense
Begin	$60,300		$25,000	$200,000		
1)		$15,000				
4)						($2,000)
6)	$ 275					
8)					($110)	
TOTAL	$60,575	$15,000	$25,000	$200,000	($110)	($2,000)

	Salary Expense	Advertising Expense	Depreciation Expense	Insurance Expense	Sales	Cost of Goods Sold	Utility Expense
1)	($15,000)						
2)		($2,400)					
3)				($2,000)			
5)					$62,000	($28,000)	
6)							($275)
7)			($1,220)				
TOTAL	($15,000)	($2,400)	($1,220)	($2,000)	$62,000	($28,000)	($275)

Pillow Soft, Inc., a manufacturer that sells goods to customers, uses the **multi-step** income statement. The income statement for the month ended February 28th follows:

Sales	$62,000
- Cost of Goods Sold	($28,000)
= Gross Profit	$34,000
Operating Expenses:	
-Advertising Expense	($ 2,400)
- Salary Expense	($15,000)
- Rent Expense	($ 2,000)
- Insurance Expense	($ 2,000)
- Depreciation Expense	($ 1,220)
- Utilities Expense	($ 275)
- Office Supplies Expense	($ 110)
= Net Earnings	$ 10,995 (assume no income tax expense)

Sales (revenue) is the price of goods or services that were provided to the customer. The value is the amount the customer is charged (price) and is expected to pay Pillow Soft, Inc. **Cost of goods sold** is the cost of the inventory that was provided to customers.

Advertising, **salary**, and **utilities expenses** are services that were provided to the company that the company paid for <u>or</u> will pay for in the future. **Rent, insurance** and **office supplies expense** are the result of the company using assets to operate the business. **Depreciation expense** is the cost of using physical long-term assets in order to provide goods or services to customers. All activity reported on the above income statement occurred during February.

Net earnings are included in retained earnings on the balance sheet.

The **balance sheet** as of February 28th reports the following:

Assets:		Liabilities:	
Cash	$121,600	Accounts Payable	$60,575
Accounts Receivable	62,000	Salaries Payable	15,000
Inventory	32,000	Total Current Liabilities	75,575
Office Supplies	190	Notes Payable	25,000
Prepaid Expenses	14,000	Total Liabilities	100,575
Total Current Assets	229,790		
		Stockholders' Equity:	
Warehouse Equipment	50,000	Common Stock	200,000
Office Furniture	15,000	Retained Earnings	10,995
Computer Equipment	18,000	Total Stockholders' Equity	210,995
- Accumulated Depreciation	(1,220)		
Net Prop, Plant, Equip.	81,780		
		Total Liabilities and	
Total Assets	$311,570	Stockholders' Equity	$311,570

7. The Statement of Stockholders' Equity

The statement of stockholders' equity reports changes to stockholders' equity accounts. Below is a simple statement of stockholders' equity.

	Common Stock Shares	Common Stock $	Paid In Capital	Treasury Stock	Retained Earnings
Balance, December 31, 2011	**10,000**	**$1,000**	**$199,000**	**($25,000)**	**$26,000**
Issued Common Stock	5,000	$ 500	$ 64,500		
Paid Dividends					($8,000)
Net Income					$32,200
Balance, December 31, 2012	**15,000**	**$1,500**	**$263,500**	**($25,000)**	**$50,200**
Repurchased Common Stock				($10,000)	
Paid Dividends					($6,000)
Net Income					$15,600
Balance, December 31, 2013	**15,000**	**$1,500**	**$263,500**	**($35,000)**	**$59,800**

The total for each account agrees to the balance sheet on the date stated. Public companies are required to provide three years of information and private companies generally state two years. The current year activity will be listed on the bottom of the statement. The description of each transaction directly with owners is listed down the left side. The amount is placed in the column of the account name that changed because of the transaction.

Issuing common stock in 2012 increased common stock by 5,000 shares, common stock dollars by $500, and paid in capital by $64,500. Dividends paid to owners reduced retained earnings by $8,000. The income statement reported earnings of $32,200. Earnings increased retained earnings.

The company purchased its own common stock in 2013 at a cost of $10,000. The company also paid $6,000 to stockholders and reported earnings of $15,600 on the income statement during 2013.

Example 7-1 presents the statement of shareholders' equity for Chipotle Mexican Grill, Inc. The statement shows the past three years, stacked one year on top of the other. Specific transactions are described on the left side. The amount is in the column of the account that was changed by the transaction. The ending balance for each year becomes the beginning balance for the next year. The totals for each account as of December 31st are the same total amounts reported on the balance sheet for the same date.

Example 7-1: CHIPOTLE MEXICAN GRILL, INC.
CONSOLIDATED STATEMENT OF SHAREHOLDERS' EQUITY (in thousands)

	Common Stock		Additional Paid-in Capital	Treasury Stock		Retained Earnings	Accumulated Other Comprehensive Income (Loss)	Total
	Shares	Amount		Shares	Amount			
Balance, December 31, 2007	32,805	$328	$489,296	—	$—	$72,486	$—	$562,110
Stock-based compensation	51	—	11,976					11,976
Stock option exercises	22	1	470					471
Excess tax benefit on stock-based compensation, net of utilization of $33			251					251
Acquisition of treasury stock				692	(30,227)			(30,227)
Comprehensive income:								
Net income						78,202		78,202
Foreign currency translation adjustment							(193)	(193)
Balance, December 31, 2008	32,878	329	501,993	692	(30,227)	150,688	(193)	622,590
Stock-based compensation	60	1	15,664					15,665
Stock option exercises	535	5	11,788					11,793
Excess tax benefit on stock-based compensation			10,435					10,435
Acquisition of treasury stock				1,298	(84,089)			(84,089)
Comprehensive income:								
Net income						126,845		126,845
Foreign currency translation adjustment							222	222
Balance, December 31, 2009	33,473	335	539,880	1,990	(114,316)	277,533	29	703,461
Stock-based compensation	166	2	22,278					22,280
Stock option exercises	320	3	17,647					17,650
Excess tax benefit on stock-based compensation			14,526					14,526
Acquisition of treasury stock				895	(126,602)			(126,602)
Comprehensive income:								
Net income						178,981		178,981
Foreign currency translation adjustment							577	577
Balance, December 31, 2010	33,959	$ 340	$594,331	2,885	$(240,918)	$ 456,514	$ 606	$810,873

84

Example 7-1 continued   CHIPOTLE MEXICAN GRILL, INC.

The statement of shareholders' equity for the year ended December 31, 2010, indicates the following transactions occurred with owners during 2010 (in thousands.)

1) The company incurred stock-based compensation expense for granting employees 166 shares of stock in the total amount of $22,280. This transaction changed common stock by $2 and additional paid in capital by $22,278.

2) The company sold 320 shares of stock to employees through the exercise of stock options and increased common stock by $3 and additional paid in capital by $17,647.

3) The company received a tax refund related to employee stock options that increased paid in capital by $14,526.

4) The company purchased 895 shares of its own stock at a cost of $126,602. Treasury stock increased for the amount paid for the stock.

5) Net income of $178,981 was reported on the income statement. Income is transferred to retained earnings at the end of the period. Retained earnings represent the cumulative earnings kept in the company since the business began.

6) The company had $577 of gains from foreign currency transactions that have not yet been reported on the income statement (other comprehensive income.)

The final balances as of December 31, 2010 for each account on the statement of stockholders' equity are the same amounts that are reported on the balance sheet as of December 31, 2010.

Common stock and capital is reported on the balance sheet and the statement of stockholders' equity at the original cash that was exchanged for ownership.

A decrease or increase in the fair market value of common stock is not reported on the statement of stockholders' equity or the balance sheet. The change in fair market value has no impact on the company; it impacts only the investors that own the common stock.

A public company's statement of stockholders' equity often reports complex transactions that are beyond the scope of this book.

Example 7-2 illustrates the relationship between the balance sheet and the statement of stockholder's equity. The stockholders' equity amounts on the balance sheet for 2009 and 2010 are the same as the final balances on the statement of stockholders' equity for each account name on the top and the bottom of the statement. The balance sheet states only the **cumulative balance** on December 31st of the year. The statement of stockholders' equity reports the **transactions that occurred during the period** and how the transaction changed the total stockholders' equity account balances reported on the balance sheet.

Walt Disney Company
CONSOLIDATED BALANCE SHEET

Equity	2010	2009
Preferred stock, $.01 par value		
Authorized — 100 million shares, Issued — none	—	—
Common stock, $.01 par value		
Authorized — 4.6 billion shares at October 2, 2010 and 3.6 billion shares at October 3, 2009		
Issued — 2.7 billion shares at October 2, 2010 and 2.6 billion shares at October 3, 2009	28,736	27,038
Retained earnings	34,327	31,033
Accumulated other comprehensive loss	(1,881)	(1,644)
	61,182	56,427
Treasury stock, at cost, 803.1 million shares at October 2, 2010 and 781.7 million shares at October 3, 2009	(23,663)	(22,693)
Total Disney Shareholder's equity	37,519	33,734
Noncontrolling interests	1,823	1,691
Total Equity	39,342	35,425
Total liabilities and equity	$ 69,206	$63,117

Walt Disney Company
CONSOLIDATED STATEMENTS OF SHAREHOLDERS' EQUITY
(in millions, except per share data)

	Equity Attributable to Disney							
	Shares	Common Stock	Retained Earnings	Accumulated Other Comprehensive Income (Loss)	Treasury Stock	Total Disney Equity	Non-controlling Interest	Total Equity
OCTOBER 3, 2009	1,861	$27,038	$31,033	$ (1,644)	$(22,693)	$33,734	$1,691	$35,425
Net income	—	—	3,963	—	—	3,963	350	4,313
Comprehensive income						3,726	338	4,064
Equity compensation activity	54	1,498	—	—	—	1,498	—	1,498
Acquisition of Marvel	59	188	—	—	1,699	1,887	90	1,977
Common stock repurchases	(80)	—	—	—	(2,669)	(2,669)	—	(2,669)
Dividends	—	9	(662)	—	—	(653)	—	(653)
Distributions and other	—	3	(7)	—	—	(4)	(296)	(300)
OCTOBER 2, 2010	1,894	$28,736	$34,327	$ (1,881)	$(23,663)	$37,519	$1,823	$39,342

86

8. The Cash Flow Statement

The cash flow statement is used by investors and creditors to understand how a company generates and uses cash. Cash receipts and payments are not reported on the other three financial statements. The cash flow statement is the only financial statement that reports the change to cash from the various transactions of the company.

The balance sheet reports what a company uses to operate the business and amounts owed. The balance sheet does not report what happened to change the amounts from last year to this year. The income statement reports the value of goods and services provided to customers and the cost to do so. This is not the same as cash received or paid. Cash may be exchanged in a different period than items are reported on the income statement.

The cash flow statement is presented in three separate sections: operating activities, investing activities, and financing activities.

Operating Activities

The operating activities section reports the amount of cash internally generated from operating the primary business of providing to customers. Cash from operations may be used to grow the company (investing activities), be returned to investors, or be used to repay debt (financing activities.)

Companies may use the <u>indirect method</u> or the <u>direct method</u> to present cash from operating activities. Both methods are acceptable under generally accepted accounting principles.

Investing Activities

The investing activities section reports cash amounts related to purchasing or selling long-term assets. Companies invest in long-term assets to operate the business or earn a return.

Financing Activities

The financing activities section reports cash amounts related to long-term liabilities and stockholders.   The two ways to obtain cash to finance operations is from borrowing and from investors.

This book will focus on how to read and understand the information presented on the cash flow statement. Preparing a cash flow statement is beyond the scope of this book.

The Indirect Method (of reporting operating activities)

The indirect method cash flow statement begins with net income using the accrual basis of accounting. Items listed between net income and cash generated from operating activities are items that were included in net income that did not require a cash exchange during the period.

The operating activities section of the indirect cash flow statement is formatted as follows:

Net income	100,000
Depreciation expense	15,000
Gain on sale of equipment	(5,000)
Stock Compensation expense	2,400
Change in current assets and liabilities	
Accounts receivable	(4,200)
Interest receivable	6,800
Accounts payable	(8,200)
Income tax payable	2,500
Cash generated from operating activities	**109,300**

The most common items that are included in net income that do not require an exchange of cash during the period are depreciation and amortization expense, stock compensation expense, and gains or losses from the sale of assets.

Depreciation and amortization expense is the allocated cost of using long-term for the period. The current period expense is not paid for in cash in the current period. Depreciation expense is added back in the cash flow statement because the expense was subtracted from net income and was not a reduction to cash. For example,

Year 1: $150,000 cash was paid for a machine. This will be reported in the investing section of the cash flow statement in year 1.

Year 1: The machine (expected to be used for 10 years with no residual value) is used to operate the business. The depreciation expense for each year is $15,000. Depreciation expense reduces net income and is not paid for in cash.

Depreciation expense is added on the cash flow statement in the operating activities section because the company has more cash than the net income the cash flow statement begins with.

A gain on sale of equipment increases net income. The gain is not the cash received from the sale; the gain is the difference in the cash received and the net cost of the equipment. The gain is subtracted on the cash flow statement because it increased net income and no cash was received. The company will have less cash than net income. For example,

A company used equipment that cost $120,000 that was expected to have a useful life of 10 years and be sold for $20,000. The estimated expense each year the equipment is used is $10,000 using the straight-line method of depreciation.

The equipment is used for 8 years. Accumulated depreciation is $80,000 at the end of year 8. The equipment is sold for $45,000 at the beginning of year 9.

The $45,000 cash received is reported on the cash flow statement in the investing section as "proceeds from sale of equipment" in the investing section for year 9.

The $120,000 cost - $80,000 accumulated depreciation = $40,000 net cost (book value.) Cash received of $45,000 is greater than the $40,000 net cost giving a $5,000 gain.

The $5,000 gain is not the cash received; however, it is an increase to net income. The gain is subtracted on the cash flow statement because it is included in the net income the statement begins with; however, cash was not received. The $5,000 is a difference in what is reported in net income and cash generated from operations.

Many companies compensate employees by selling employees the company's common stock at a price that is lower than fair market value after the employees have worked for a stated number of years. The cost of paying the employees using stock is allocated over the years the employee works to earn the stock and is called **stock compensation expense.**

Stock compensation expense is subtracted on the income statement when determining net income. The expense is paid in stock and is not paid in cash. The amount is added on the cash flow statement because no cash is paid and therefore; the company has more cash than net income.

The income statement compares to the operating section of the cash flow statement as follows:

Income Statement		Cash From Operations:	
Revenue	$ 100,000	Net Income	$27,600
- Expenses Paid in Cash	($ 60,000)	Depreciation Expense	$15,000
- Depreciation Expense	($ 15,000)	Stock Option Expense	$ 2,400
- Stock Option Expense	($ 2,400)	Gain on Sale of Assets	($5,000)
+ Gain on Sale of Assets	$ 5,000		
= Net Income	$ 27,600	Cash from Operations:	$40,000

The company has more cash than net income because depreciation expense and stock option expense were not paid in cash and the gain was not cash received during the current period.

The change in current assets and current liabilities represents the difference in the revenue and expense that was reported on the income statement and the cash that was exchanged during the period.

An increase in accounts receivable (or any current asset) is a decrease on the cash flow statement because less cash was received than revenues. A decrease in accounts receivable (or any current asset) is an increase on the cash flow statement because more cash was collected than revenues.

	Reported on the Income Statement	Reported on the Balance Sheet	Difference in Cash and Net Income: Cash Flow Statement
Revenues	$100,000		
Prior year accounts receivable balance		$20,000	
Current year accounts receivable balance		$24,200	($4,200)

Accounts receivable increased when less cash was received than the revenue reported on the income statement for the period. The cash flow statement begins with net income. The amount not yet received is deducted from net income to determine cash from operations during the period.

An decrease in accounts payable (or any current liability) is a decrease on the cash flow statement because more cash was paid than the expense and therefore the company has less cash than net income. An increase in accounts payable (or any current liability) is an increase on the cash flow statement because the expense was not paid and therefore the company has more cash than net income.

	Reported on the Income Statement	Reported on the Balance Sheet	Difference in Cash and Net Income: Cash Flow Statement
Expenses	$50,000		
Prior year accounts payable balance		$30,000	
Current year accounts payable balance		$21,800	($8,200)

Accounts payable decreases when more cash is paid than expenses reported on the income statement for the period. The cash flow statement begins with net income. More cash was paid than expenses included in net income and the additional cash that was paid reduces the cash generated from operations during the period.

90

The cash flow statement reports the change in current assets and current liabilities as follows:

	Increase	Decrease
Current Asset:	Negative Number	Positive Number
Current Liability:	Positive Number	Negative Number

Non cash expenses and losses are added back to net income to get cash generated.

Non cash revenues and gains are deducted from net income to get cash generated.

Further discussion of how the indirect method operating activities section is prepared and other items presented in the operating section (such as deferred taxes) is beyond the scope of this book. The key thing to understand is that all items listed in the operating activities section were included in net income on the income statement and there was no related exchange of cash.

The Direct Method (of reporting operating activities)

This format directly states the amount of cash that was collected and the amount of cash that was paid for specific items during the period.

All amounts stated represent the cash received or paid and the format is as follows:

Cash collected from customers	248,500
Cash collected related to investments	6,500
Cash paid for inventory	(62,600)
Cash paid for salaries	(39,100)
Cash paid for income taxes	(22,900)
Cash paid for interest	(8,300)
Cash paid for other expenses	(12,800)
Cash generated from operating activities	**109,300**

The direct method is much easier for non accountants to understand. It allows for period to period comparisons of cash received or cash paid. The FASB and the IASB currently favor the direct method; however, almost all companies in the United States currently use the indirect method because accounting records are maintained using the accrual basis of accounting. The accrual basis of accounting does not record revenues and expenses when cash is exchanged.

Total cash from operating activities will be the same using the direct and the indirect method.

The investing and financing sections of the cash flow statement are reported using one format.

The **investing activity section** reports the cash exchanged from the **purchase or sale of long-term assets.** The amount reported on the cash flow statement is the cash exchanged.

An example of an investing activity section is presented below:

Proceeds from selling equipment	150,000
Purchases of equipment	(36,000)
Cash generated from investing activities	114,000

The beginning (prior year) and ending (current year) balances of long-term assets are reported on the balance sheet. The balance sheet does not report what occurred to change the amounts from one period to the next. Amounts reported on the cash flow statement relate to the change in the balance sheet amounts for long-term assets as follows:

	Balance Sheet Equipment Account	The Investing Section Reports the Exchange of Cash ONLY
Prior Year Balance	$300,000	
+Purchased Equipment:		
With Borrowings	$ 60,000	
Paid Cash	$ 36,000	($36,000)
- Sold Equipment:		
Cost of Equipment	($200,000)	
Cash Received		$150,000
Current Year Balance:	$196,000	

Amounts paid for purchases and amounts received from sales are NOT netted on the cash flow statement (except for investments intended to be purchased and sold many times during the year.)

Cash paid for property, plant, and equipment is often called **capital expenditures** in the investing section of the cash flow statement.

The **financing activity section** reports the cash exchanged from **borrowing or repaying long-term debt and cash exchanged with owners.** The amount reported on the cash flow statement is the cash exchanged.

An example of a financing activity section is presented below:

Proceeds from borrowing long-term debt	15,000
Repayment of long-term debt	(225,000)
Proceeds from issuing common stock	50,000
Dividend payments	(25,000)
Cash generated from/(used for) financing activities	(185,000)

The beginning (prior year) and ending (current year) balances of long-term liabilities and stockholders' equity accounts are reported on the balance sheet. The balance sheet does not report what occurred to change the amounts from one period to the next. Amounts reported on the cash flow statement relate to the change in the balance sheet amounts as follows:

	Balance Sheet L/T Notes Payable Account	The Financing Section Reports the Exchange of Cash ONLY
Prior Year Balance	$500,000	
New Cash Borrowings	$ 15,000	$ 15,000
Payments on Borrowings	($225,000)	($225,000)
Purchased Land with Debt	$100,000	
Current Year Balance	$390,000	

Cash was not received when the company borrowed to purchase land; land was received. Only cash amounts received or paid are reported on the cash flow statement. Non cash exchanges of long-term items are reported at the bottom of the cash flow statement.

	Balance Sheet Common Stock Account	The Financing Section Reports the Exchange of Cash
Beginning Balance	$700,000	
Issued Stock	$ 50,000	$ 50,000
Ending Balance	$750,000	

Dividend payments are a very common cash exchange between the owners and the company. Cash dividends reduce retained earnings on the balance sheet.

A complete cash flow statement is presented on the following page in **Example 8-1.**

The cash flow statement provides valuable insight into a company's strategy that cannot be seen by looking at the other financial statements. Common general strategies are as follows:

1) Use excess cash for investments in stock or bonds.

2) Grow the company through the purchase of long-term assets.

3) Grow the company through the purchase of other companies.

4) Use cash generated from operations to grow the company.

5) Finance growth through borrowing from banks or investors.

6) Finance growth through issuing stock to owners.

7) Keep earnings in the company to use for growth or consistently
pay investors a return on their investment (dividends.)

Example 8-1 provides a cash flow statement that reveals some of the important things that should be noted when reading a cash flow statement.

Net income	100,000
Depreciation expense	15,000
Gain on sale of equipment	(5,000)
Stock Compensation expense	2,400
Change in current assets and liabilities	
Accounts receivable	(4,200)
Inventory	6,800
Accounts payable	(8,200)
Income tax payable	2,500
Cash generated from operating activities	109,300
Proceeds from selling equipment	150,000
Purchases of equipment	(36,000)
Cash generated from investing activities	114,000
Proceeds from borrowing from banks	15,000
Repayment of loans to banks	(225,000)
Proceeds from issuing common stock	50,000
Dividends paid	(25,000)
Cash generated from financing activities	(185,000)
Total change in cash	38,300

Example 8-1 continued:

The following strategy of the company is revealed by the cash flow statement:

1) Positive cash flow from operations gives the company financial flexibility to invest to grow, repay liabilities, or return cash to investors.

2) Small changes in current assets and current liabilities compared to net income are normal and indicate customers are generally paying the company and expenses are generally being paid timely. Large changes would indicate otherwise.

3) The cost of using assets (depreciation expense) is $18,000 and the company paid $36,000 for new equipment. The company is purchasing more long-term assets than is currently being used up. This indicates the company is attempting to grow.

4) The proceeds from selling equipment were used to repay long-term debt. Investors and creditors will wonder why the company sold such a significant amount of assets and if the company has the ability to generate enough cash to repay amounts due in the near future.

5) The company raised money from investors by issuing common stock. This money appears to have been used to repay loans. Less debt generally strengthens the future financial position.

6) A fairly significant portion of net income is paid to investors (dividends.)

Free cash flow indicates the company's ability to generate more cash than is necessary to pay for daily operations (including replacing long-term assets.) Free cash flow may be defined in various ways; however, the most common definition is as follows:

  Cash Flow from Operating Activities
- Capital Expenditures for Long-term Assets
- Dividends Paid to Stockholders
= Free Cash Flow

The free cash flow for the company in Example 8-1 is as follows:

Cash Flow from Operating Activities	109,300
- Capital Expenditures for Long-term Assets	(36,000)
- Dividends Paid to Stockholders	(25,000)
= Free Cash Flow	48,300

Free cash flow can be used to pay long-term liabilities or invest in additional long-term assets. A low amount of free cash flow often hinders the ability to borrow and could make future growth difficult.

Free cash flow and the average amount that must be repaid each year is often used to determine a company's ability to repay debt. This is referred to as **cash flow adequacy** and is computed as follows:

$$\text{Cash flow adequacy} = \frac{\text{Free Cash Flow}}{\text{Average Amount of Debt Maturing over the Next Five Years}}$$

The cash flow adequacy ratio indicates how many times the company's cash flow is able to repay long-term debt as it comes due. A ratio higher than 2.0 generally indicates a company has the ability to repay its debt.

The amount of debt that must be repaid each year for the next five years must be disclosed in the footnotes and is used to determine the average amount that must be repaid each year.

Example 8-2 presents the statement of cash flows for the retailer, Target Corporation. The statement is separated into the three sections: operations, investing, and financing. The company uses the indirect method that begins with net income and adjusts for items that are included in income and cash was not received or paid during the period.

Target's free cash flow for 2010 is as follows:

	Cash Flow from Operating Activities	$ 5,271
-	Capital Expenditures for Long-term Assets	(2,129)
-	Dividends Paid to Stockholders	(609)
=	Free Cash Flow	$ 2,533

The footnotes of Target Corporation report the following amounts of debt due to repaid in the next five years.

2011	$ 106
2012	2,251
2013	3,816
2014	1
2015	27
Total	$ 6,201

$6,201 / 5 Years = $1,240 five year average

Target's cash flow adequacy is $\dfrac{\$2,533}{\$1,240} = 2.04$ times

Target should have the ability to repay debt as it becomes due in the future as long as earnings continue to be consistent or improve.

Example 8-2 continued:

Target Corporation: Consolidated Statements of Cash Flows

(millions)	2010	2009	2008
Operating activities			
Net earnings	$2,920	$2,488	$2,214
Reconciliation to cash flow			
Depreciation and amortization	2,084	2,023	1,826
Share-based compensation expense	109	103	72
Deferred income taxes	445	364	91
Bad debt expense	528	1,185	1,251
Non-cash (gains)/losses and other, net	(145)	143	316
Changes in operating accounts:			
Accounts receivable originated at Target	(78)	(57)	(458)
Inventory	(417)	(474)	77
Other current assets	(124)	(129)	(99)
Other noncurrent assets	(212)	(114)	(55)
Accounts payable	115	174	(389)
Accrued and other current liabilities	149	257	(230)
Other noncurrent liabilities	(103)	(82)	(186)
Cash flow provided by operations	5,271	5,881	4,430
Investing activities			
Expenditures for property and equipment	(2,129)	(1,729)	(3,547)
Proceeds from disposal of property and equipment	69	33	39
Change in accounts receivable originated at third parties	363	(10)	(823)
Other investments	(47)	3	(42)
Cash flow required for investing activities	(1,744)	(1,703)	(4,373)
Financing activities			
Reductions of short-term notes payable	—	—	(500)
Additions to long-term debt	1,011	—	3,557
Reductions of long-term debt	(2,259)	(1,970)	(1,455)
Dividends paid	(609)	(496)	(465)
Repurchase of stock	(2,452)	(423)	(2,815)
Stock option exercises and related tax benefit	294	47	43
Other	—	—	(8)
Cash flow required for financing activities	(4,015)	(2,842)	(1,643)
Net increase/(decrease) in cash and cash equivalents	(488)	1,336	(1,586)
Cash and cash equivalents at beginning of year	2,200	864	2,450
Cash and cash equivalents at end of year	$1,712	$2,200	$864

Example 8-2 continued

The cash flow statement of Target Corporation reveals the following:

1) Cash flow from operations is higher than net income because depreciation and amortization expense deducted from earnings is not paid in the current period. This expense was paid with cash in a prior period when the assets were purchased. Purchases of long-term assets are reported in the investing section. Eventually, cash will have to be used in future periods to purchase new long-term assets to replace the assets used.

Expenditures for property and equipment in 2009 and 2010 are approximately equal to depreciation expense. This indicates the company replaced assets and did not attempt to grow during these two years. Expenditures for property and equipment in 2008 were almost double depreciation expense. The company took steps to grow the business in 2008.

2) Share based compensation and bad debt expense reduced net income; however, these expenses are not paid with cash. Bad debt expense was higher in 2008 and 2009 during a down-turn in the economy.

3) The amounts of the changes in operating accounts are typical and indicate nothing unusual related to collecting from customers or paying expenses. Routine cash flow management often results in minor swings in current liabilities. A user should notice any large changes in accounts receivable that indicate customers are not paying timely, large increases in payables that indicate invoices are not being paid timely or large changes in inventory that might indicate inventory is not selling as quickly.

4) The company borrowed long-term debt of $3.557 billion in 2008. This was most likely used to help pay for the purchase of property and equipment in 2008. Additional borrowings in 2010 of $1,011were most likely used to purchase long-term assets or repay debt or purchase treasury stock.

5) The company paid about 21% of earnings to owners as dividends. The company has a history of returning cash to owners. The dividend amount has grown consistently over the past three years.

6) The company has paid almost $5.7 billion to purchase its own stock in the past three years. This indicates the company believes no investment is available that gives a higher return on investment than purchasing its own stock and reducing the number of outstanding shares. Less outstanding shares gives higher earnings per share which often results in a higher fair market value per share.

7) Cash has almost doubled from 2008 to 2010. Cash amounts related to other investments is very small (investing section.) This indicates the company does not have significant investments in addition to cash on hand. The cash balance is the majority of available funds.

8) The company uses more than a third of cash generated from operations to repay long-term debt. Net earnings are only slightly higher than the debt repaid in 2010. The reader should look at the footnotes and note the amount of debt that must be repaid in the near future. Repayment of debt could impact the ability to purchase treasury stock, pay dividends, or grow the company in the future.

9. Footnotes and Other Information

The four financial statements are summary reports that do not present <u>all</u> the detail information necessary to make sound business decisions. Footnotes are provided along with the financial statements to provide other information that could make a difference when making a decision to invest or lend money. Generally accepted accounting principles require footnotes to be provided for all years presented on the financial statements. *footnotes are required*

Footnotes are numbered (or lettered) and a standard order of presenting information is generally followed. The footnotes general begin with a brief description of the company and a description of the accounting methods used to prepare the financial statements. This is followed by a description of mergers or acquisitions; followed by discussion of additional information related to assets, liabilities, and stockholders' equity.

The examples provided below are taken from the footnotes of the Walt Disney Company 2011 Form 10-K filed with the Securities Exchange Commission. (The financial statements of Walt Disney Company are provided in chapter 1.)

A sample of information provided in footnote 1 of Walt Disney Company follows:

1 Description of the Business and Segment Information

The Walt Disney Company, together with the subsidiaries through which businesses are conducted (the Company), is a diversified worldwide entertainment company with operations in the following business segments: Media Networks, Parks and Resorts, Studio Entertainment, Consumer Products and Interactive Media.

Media Networks

The Company operates through consolidated subsidiaries the ESPN, Disney Channels Worldwide, ABC Family and SOAPnet cable television networks. The Company also operates the ABC Television Network and eight owned television stations, as well as the ESPN Radio Network and Radio Disney Network (the Radio Networks) and 35 owned and operated radio stations. Both the ABC Television Network and Radio Networks have affiliated stations providing coverage to households throughout the United States. The Company also produces original television programming for network, first-run syndication, pay, and international television markets, along with original animated television programming for network, pay, and international syndication markets. The Company has interests in joint ventures that operate programming services and are accounted for under the equity method, including AETN/Lifetime. Additionally, the Company operates ABC-, ESPN-, ABC Family- and SOAPnet-branded

Reporting Period

The Company's fiscal year ends on the Saturday closest to September 30 and consists of fifty-two weeks with the exception that approximately every six years, we have a fifty-three week year. When a fifty-three week year occurs, the Company reports the additional week in the fourth quarter. Fiscal 2009 was a fifty-three week year beginning on September 28, 2008 and ending on October 3, 2009.

Use of Estimates

The preparation of financial statements in conformity with generally accepted accounting principles requires management to make estimates and assumptions that affect the amounts reported in the financial statements and footnotes thereto. Actual results may differ from those estimates.

Revenue Recognition - when rev is recognized

Broadcast advertising revenues are recognized when commercials are aired. Revenues from television subscription services related to the Company's primary cable programming services are recognized as services are provided. Certain of the Company's contracts with cable and satellite operators include annual live programming commitments. In these cases, recognition of revenues subject to the commitments is deferred until the annual commitments are satisfied, which generally results in higher revenue recognition in the second half of the year.

Revenues from advance theme park ticket sales are recognized when the tickets are used. For non-expiring, multi-day tickets, revenues are recognized over a four-year time period based on estimated usage, which is derived from historical usage patterns.

Revenues from the theatrical distribution of motion pictures are recognized when motion pictures are exhibited. Revenues from DVD and video game sales, net of anticipated returns and customer incentives, are recognized on the date that video units are made available for sale by retailers. Revenues from the licensing of feature films and television programming are recorded when the content is available for telecast by the licensee and when certain other conditions are met.

Merchandise licensing advances and guarantee royalty payments are recognized based on the contractual royalty rate when the licensed product is sold by the licensee. Non-refundable advances and minimum guarantee royalty payments in excess of royalties earned are generally recognized as revenue at the end of the contract term. Revenues from our internet and mobile operations are recognized as services are rendered. Advertising revenues at our internet operations are recognized when advertisements are viewed online.

Allowance for Doubtful Accounts - uncollectable recievables

The Company maintains an allowance for doubtful accounts to reserve for potentially uncollectible receivables. The allowance for doubtful accounts is estimated based on our analysis of trends in overall receivables aging, specific identification of certain receivables that are at risk of not being paid, past collection experience and current economic trends. In times of domestic or global economic turmoil, the Company's estimates and judgments with respect to the collectability of its receivables are subject to greater uncertainty than in more stable periods.

Advertising Expense

Advertising costs are expensed as incurred. Advertising expense for fiscal 2011, 2010, and 2009 was $2.8 billion, $2.6 billion, and $2.7 billion, respectively.

100

Investments

Debt securities that the Company has the positive intent and ability to hold to maturity are classified as "held-to maturity" and reported at amortized cost. Debt securities not classified as held-to-maturity and marketable equity securities are classified as either "trading" or "available-for-sale." Trading and available-for-sale securities are recorded at fair value with unrealized gains and losses included in earnings or accumulated other comprehensive income/(loss), respectively. All other equity securities are accounted for using either the cost method or the equity method.

The Company regularly reviews its investments to determine whether a decline in fair value below the cost basis is other than temporary. If the decline in fair value is determined to be other than temporary, the cost basis of the investment is written down to fair value.

Parks, Resorts and Other Property - what cost method they use; type of depreciation

Parks, resorts, and other property are carried at historical cost. Depreciation is computed on the straight-line method over estimated useful lives as follows:

Attractions	25 – 40 years
Buildings and improvements	20 – 40 years
Leasehold improvements	Life of lease or asset life if less
Land improvements	20 – 40 years
Furniture, fixtures and equipment	3 – 25 years

Other Intangible Assets

Amortizable intangible assets are generally amortized on a straight-line basis over periods up to 40 years. The costs to periodically renew our intangible assets are expensed as incurred. The Company has determined that there are currently no legal, competitive, economic or other factors that materially limit the useful life of our FCC licenses and trademarks. The Company expects its aggregate annual amortization expense for existing amortizable intangible assets for fiscal years 2012 through 2016 to be as follows:

2012	$ 176
2013	$ 156
2014	$ 119
2015	$ 110
2016	$ 106

Employee Compensation – Retirement Benefits

In September 2006, the FASB issued guidance that requires recognition of the overfunded or underfunded status of defined benefit pension and other postretirement plans as an asset or liability in the statement of financial position and changes in that funded status to be recognized in comprehensive income in the year in which the changes occur. The guidance on retirement benefits also requires measurement of the funded status of a plan as of the end of the fiscal year. The Company adopted the recognition provision in fiscal year 2007 which resulted in a $261 million charge to accumulated other comprehensive income. The Company adopted the measurement date provision by remeasuring plan assets and benefit obligations at the beginning of fiscal 2009. Adoption of the measurement date provisions resulted in a reduction of $35 million to retained earnings and a $100 million benefit to accumulated other comprehensive income.

Footnote 2 provides a description of mergers and acquisitions or other significant changes to the business. A sample of information provided by Walt Disney Company follows:

UTH Russia Limited

On November 18, 2011, the Company acquired a 49% ownership interest in the Seven TV network from UTH Russia Limited (UTH) for $300 million. The Seven TV network will be converted to an ad-supported, free-to air Disney Channel in Russia.

UTV

On May 9, 2008, the Company acquired a 24% interest (bringing its undiluted interest to 37%) in UTV Software Communications Limited (UTV), a media company headquartered and publicly traded in India, for approximately $197 million. In accordance with Indian securities regulations, the Company was required to make an open tender offer to purchase up to an additional 23% of UTV's publicly traded voting shares for a price equivalent to the May 9th, 2008 Indian rupee purchase price. In November 2008, the Company completed the open offer and acquired an incremental 23% of UTV's voting shares for approximately $138 million bringing its undiluted interest to 60%. UTV's founder has a four-year option which expires in November 2012 to buy all or a portion of the shares acquired by the Company during the open-offer period at a price no less than the Company's open-offer price.

Playdom

On August 27, 2010, the Company acquired Playdom, Inc. (Playdom), a company that develops online social games. This acquisition is designed to strengthen the Company's digital gaming portfolio and provide access to a new customer base. Total consideration was approximately $563 million, subject to certain conditions and adjustments, of which approximately $108 million is subject to vesting conditions and recognized as post-close compensation expense. Additional consideration of up to $200 million may be paid if Playdom achieves predefined revenues and earnings targets for calendar year 2012. The Company has recognized the fair value (determined by a probability weighting of the potential payouts) of the additional consideration as a liability and subsequent changes in the estimate of fair value up to the ultimate amount to be paid, will be recognized in earnings.

Miramax

On December 3, 2010, the Company sold Miramax Film NY, LLC (Miramax) for $663 million. Net proceeds which reflect closing adjustments, the settlement of related claims and obligations and Miramax's cash balance at closing were $532 million, resulting in a pre-tax gain of $64 million, which is reported in "Other income" in the fiscal 2011 Consolidated Statement of Income. The book value of Miramax included $217 million of allocated goodwill that is not deductible for tax purposes. Accordingly, tax expense recorded in connection with the transaction was approximately $103 million resulting in an after tax loss of $39 million.

Footnote 3 begins a series of footnotes that provide the details for items reported on the balance sheet and the income statement. Information is also provided for items not reported on the financial statements.

6 Investments

Investments consist of the following:

	October 1, 2011	October 2, 2010
Investments, equity basis(1)	$ 2,052	$ 2,123
Investments, other	346	354
Investment in aircraft leveraged leases	37	36
	$ 2,435	$ 2,513

(1) Equity investments consist of investments in companies over which the Company has significant influence but not the majority of the equity or risks and rewards.

7 International Theme Park Investments

The Company has a 51% effective ownership interest in the operations of Disneyland Paris, a 47% ownership interest in the operations of Hong Kong Disneyland Resort and a 43% ownership interest in the operations of Shanghai Disney Resort, all of which are VIEs and are consolidated in the Company's financial statements.

8 Film and Television Costs

	October 1, 2011	October 2, 2010
Theatrical film costs		
Released, less amortization	$ 1,580	$ 1,551
Completed, not released	3	290
In-process	1,198	1,325
In development or pre-production	175	138
	2,956	3,304
Television costs		
Released, less amortization	688	790
Completed, not released	259	164
In-process	231	153
In development or pre-production	0	6
	1,178	1,113
Television broadcast rights	897	1,034
Total Film and Television Costs	5,031	5,451

11 Pension and Other Benefit Programs

The Company maintains pension and postretirement medical benefit plans covering most of its employees not covered by union or industry-wide plans. Employees generally hired after January 1, 1994 and employees generally hired after January 1, 1987 for certain of our media businesses are not eligible for postretirement medical benefits. With respect to its defined benefit pension plans, the Company's policy is to fund, at a minimum, the amount necessary on an actuarial basis to provide for benefits in accordance with the requirements of the Employee Retirement Income Security Act of 1974, as amended by the Pension Protection Act of 2006 (PPA). Pension benefits are generally based on years of service and/or compensation.

Plan Funded Status and Plan Contributions

The projected benefit obligation, accumulated benefit obligation and aggregate fair value of plan assets for pension plans with accumulated benefit obligations in excess of plan assets were $8.7 billion, $8.1 billion and $5.7 billion, respectively, as of October 1, 2011 and $7.3 billion, $6.8 billion and $4.9 billion as of October 2, 2010, respectively. For pension plans with projected benefit obligations in excess of plan assets, the projected benefit obligation and aggregate fair value of plan assets were $8.7 billion and $5.7 billion, respectively, as of October 1, 2011 and $7.3 billion and $4.9 billion as of October 2, 2010, respectively.

During fiscal 2011, the Company made contributions to its pension and postretirement medical plans totaling $935 million, which included discretionary contributions above the minimum requirements for pension plans. The Company currently expects pension and postretirement medical plan contributions in fiscal 2012 to total approximately $325 million to $375 million.

14 Detail of Certain Balance Sheet Accounts

	October 1, 2011	October 2, 2010
Current receivables		
Accounts receivable	$ 5,947	$ 5,454
Other	496	656
Allowance for doubtful accounts	(261)	(326)
	$ 6,182	$ 5,784
Other current assets		
Prepaid expenses	$ 449	$ 446
Other	185	135
	$ 634	$ 581
Parks, resorts and other property, at cost		
Attractions, buildings and improvements	$ 17,662	$ 15,998
Leasehold improvements	650	644
Furniture, fixtures and equipment	13,476	12,575
Land improvements	3,727	3,658
	35,515	32,875
Accumulated depreciation	(19,572)	(18,373)
Projects in progress	2,625	2,180
Land	1,127	1,124
	$ 19,695	$ 17,806
Intangible assets		
Copyrights and other character intangibles	$ 3,202	$ 3,118
Other amortizable intangible assets	501	352
Accumulated amortization	(542)	(360)
Net amortizable intangible assets	3,161	3,110
FCC licenses	722	733
Trademarks	1,218	1,218
Other indefinite lived intangible assets	20	20
	$ 5,121	$ 5,081
Other non-current assets		
Receivables	$ 1,683	$ 1,275
Prepaid expenses	177	127
Other	754	1,306
	$ 2,614	$ 2,708
Accounts payable and other accrued liabilities		
Accounts payable	$ 4,546	$ 4,413
Payroll and employee benefits	1,468	1,484
Other	348	212
	$ 6,362	6,109
Other long-term liabilities		
Deferred revenues	$ 233	$ 244
Capital lease obligations	288	224
Program licenses and rights	99	206
Participation and residual liabilities	342	415
Pension and postretirement medical liabilities	4,223	3,378
Other	1,610	1,637
	$ 6,795	$ 6,104

Other items commonly discussed in the footnotes are:

1) the detail of long-term debt and when amounts are due to be repaid

2) the details of employee retirement liabilities and healthcare benefit liabilities

3) how earnings per share is calculated

4) stock option compensation related to employees

5) pending legal situations

6) the performance of each segment of the business

FASB provides guidelines for the types of information and the level of detail that must be provided in the footnotes. Companies are required to state any information that is expected to make a difference in a decision to invest or lend money.

Public companies in the United States are required to provide periodic reports to the Securities and Exchange Commission (SEC). All reports filed with the SEC are public information and can be accessed at www.sec.gov Companies also provide their SEC reports, press releases, and other information on the investor relations pages of their website. See chapter 1 for additional discussion related to the SEC.

Public companies must provide a **10-K** for each fiscal year to the SEC. The 10-K typically reports the most comprehensive information available in the following required order:

Item 1:	Business Operations
Item 1A:	Risk Factors
Item 2:	Properties
Item 3:	Legal Proceedings
Item 4:	Directors and Executive Officers of the Registrant
Item 5:	Market for Registrants Common Stock and Related Stockholder Matters
Item 6:	Selected Financial Data (generally 5 years of summarized data)
Item 7:	Management's Discussion and Analysis of Financial Condition and Results of Operations (a comparison of the current year to prior years)
Item 7A:	Qualitative and Quantitative Disclosure about Market Risk
Item 8:	Auditor's Reports, Financial Statements and Footnotes
Item 9:	Changes in and Disagreements with Accountants on Accounting and Financial Disclosure

Item 1 provides a detail explanation of the company's products and services along with a discussion of the general business operations. Item 7 provides management's perspective of the current year compared to prior years. The SEC requires management to share their knowledge of the company and their expectations of future performance; however, companies are hesitant to state future expectations due to the legal risks associated with incorrect projections.

The SEC requires various other reports to be filed during the year and as significant events occur.   A few of the more common reports are discussed below:

The **Form 8-K** is used to announce significant events. Examples of significant events are: mergers or acquisitions, borrowing significant additional funds, hiring or terminating executive officers, election to the board of directors, and significant legal actions.

The **Form 14A** provides information about executive officers and their compensation along with items common stockholders will vote on.

The **Form S-1** is used to provide information to investors before the initial public offering of stock.

The **Form 10-Q** provides quarterly financial information.

The Form **20-F** is an annual report similar to the 10-K that is used by foreign companies with shares that trade on public stock markets in the United States.

Public companies also provide an **annual report** to investors. This report is used as a marketing document.   It begins with a letter to stockholders from the chief executive officer summarizing the company's major achievements for the year. It is usually very colorful with many charts and graphs of positive data. The annual report includes the financial statements and footnotes.

The SEC was established to protect the interest of investors that own publicly traded companies only. Private companies that do not trade shares of ownership on a public stock exchange are not required to file reports with the SEC. Private companies generally provide financial statements and footnotes quarterly and annually only to their specific investors or lenders as requested.

10. Financial Statement Analysis

Financial statement analysis consists of the examination of the relationships among financial statements and trends over time. Financial statement analysis is performed to discover strengths and weaknesses of a company for the purpose of projecting future performance and the ability to repay borrowings (debt.)

Financial statement analysis is not done by the accountant; it is done by investors and creditors to help them make a decision on how to best use their excess money.   Guidelines for financial statement analysis are not provided by generally accepted accounting principles. Investors and creditors generally do the following prior to making financial decisions:

1) Analyze financial information for <u>one company</u> to discover relationships and trends.

2) A comparison of <u>one company to another company</u> in order to determine which company may provide the highest return on investment.

It is difficult to draw conclusions when doing financial statement analysis without a basis of comparison. It is uncertain whether net income of $1 million is impressive until one knows total sales in the same period. If sales were $2 million, $1 million net income seems excellent. If sales were $2 billion, $1 million net income seems very lacking. However, $1 million in net income for a company might be a solid performance if all other companies in the same industry are losing significant amounts of money. The size of a company (total sales and total assets) and the industry the business operates in must be considered when doing financial statement analysis.

Financial statement analysis is done by various financial decision makers to evaluate a company's future profitability and risks.

Decision Makers:	Decisions:
Equity Investors	What are profits expected to be in future years? What are the risks to future profits? Is the stock priced appropriately for appreciation?
Creditors	Should credit be extended? How much credit should be extended? What terms of credit should be extended? What interest rate is appropriate? What is the level of risk of repayment?

Decision Makers:	Decisions:
Board of Directors	Is the management team performing? Are managers fairly compensated? Do the financial statements fairly reflect the business? Is the amount of dividends paid appropriate?
Managers	How do we compare with others in our industry? Should we acquire or divest? Should we repurchase our own stock? Is cash flow sufficient to support operations and long-term growth?
Auditors	What is the likelihood the financial statements are misstated?
Regulatory Agencies	What is the likelihood the financial statements are misstated? Are regulated companies' rates appropriate? Did the company pay the appropriate amount of taxes?

The two most common methods of financial statement analysis are as follows:

1) **Common size analysis** uses percentages to compare the results of different periods to identify trends over time <u>for one company</u>.

2) **Ratio analysis** compares one company to another company or the industry average to determine which company has the ability to generate stronger profits, has a stronger financial position, or may generate a higher return on investment.

Common Size Analysis

Common size analysis is done to compare the results of operations and the financial position of one company over more than one period of time. All amounts are viewed as a percentage of total assets (balance sheet) or total sales (income statement.)

A common size income statement allows the user to determine if the company's expenses and earnings are changing at a rate that is consistent with changes in revenues. A common size balance sheet allows the user to determine if different assets or liabilities are changing in proportion to the total size of the company.

Example 10-1 presents a common size income statement for Intel Corporation. The percentages out to the side are a percent of total net revenue for the year. Higher sales, higher gross profit, and a lower percent for expenses from one year to the next are generally perceived as positive trends.

INTEL CORPORATION
CONSOLIDATED STATEMENTS OF INCOME

Three Years Ended December 25, 2010

(In Millions, Except Per Share Amounts)	2010		2009		2008	
Net revenue	43,623	100.0%	35,127	100.0%	37,586	100.0%
Cost of sales	15,132	34.7%	15,566	44.3%	16,742	44.5%
Gross margin	28,491	65.3%	19,561	55.7%	20,844	55.5%
Research and development	6,576	15.1%	5,653	16.1%	5,722	15.2%
Marketing, general and administrative	6,309	14.5%	7,931	22.6%	5,452	14.5%
Restructuring and asset impairment charges	0	0.0%	231	0.7%	710	1.9%
Amortization of acquisition-related intangibles	18	0.0%	35	0.1%	6	0.0%
Operating expenses	12,903	29.6%	13,850	39.4%	11,890	31.6%
Operating income	15,588	35.7%	5,711	16.3%	8,954	23.8%
Gains (losses) on equity method investments, net	117	0.3%	(147)	-0.4%	(1,380)	-3.7%
Gains (losses) on other equity investments, net	231	0.5%	(23)	-0.1%	(376)	-1.0%
Interest and other, net	109	0.2%	163	0.5%	488	1.3%
Income before taxes	16,045	36.8%	5,704	16.2%	7,686	20.4%
Provision for taxes	4,581	10.5%	1,335	3.8%	2,394	6.4%
Net income	11,461	26.3%	4,369	12.4%	5,292	14.1%

Example 10-1 continued:

The common size income statement for Intel Corporation reveals the following:

1. Cost of sales were significantly lower in 2010 compared to prior years. This is a key factor that led to higher operating income and higher net income.
2. Intel consistently invested in research and development as sales fluctuated.
3. Intel incurred higher marketing, general and administration costs during 2009 compared to sales when sales were slowing. This may have led to the increase in sales in 2010.

Example 10-2 presents a common size balance sheet for Intel Corporation. The percentages out to the side are a percent of total assets at the end of the year.

INTEL CORPORATION
CONSOLIDATED BALANCE SHEETS

December 25, 2010 and December 26, 2009

(In Millions, Except Par Value)	2010		2009	
Assets				
Cash and cash equivalents	5,498	8.7%	3,987	7.5%
Short-term investments	11,294	17.9%	5,285	10.0%
Trading assets	5,093	8.1%	4,648	8.8%
Accounts receivable, net of allowance	2,867	4.5%	2,273	4.3%
for doubtful accounts of $28 ($19 in 2009)				
Inventories	3,757	5.9%	2,935	5.5%
Deferred tax assets	1,488	2.4%	1,216	2.3%
Other current assets	1,614	2.6%	813	1.5%
Total current assets	**31,611**	50.0%	**21,157**	39.8%
Property, plant and equipment, net	17,899	28.3%	17,225	32.4%
Marketable equity securities	1,008	1.6%	773	1.5%
Other long-term investments	3,026	4.8%	4,179	7.9%
Goodwill	4,531	7.2%	4,421	8.3%
Other long-term assets	5,111	8.1%	5,340	10.1%
Total assets	**63,186**	100.0%	**53,095**	100.0%
Liabilities and stockholders' equity				
Short-term debt	38	0.1%	172	0.3%
Accounts payable	2,290	3.6%	1,883	3.5%
Accrued compensation and benefits	2,888	4.6%	2,448	4.6%
Accrued advertising	1,007	1.6%	773	1.5%
Deferred income on shipments to distributors	622	1.0%	593	1.1%
Other accrued liabilities	2,482	3.9%	1,722	3.2%
Total current liabilities	**9,327**	14.8%	**7,591**	14.3%

Example 10-2 Intel Corporation
Balance Sheet (continued)

(In Millions, Except Par Value)	2010		2009	
Long-term income taxes payable	190	0.3%	193	0.4%
Long-term debt	**2,077**	3.3%	**2,049**	3.9%
Long-term deferred tax liabilities	**926**	1.5%	**555**	1.0%
Other long-term liabilities	**1,236**	2.0%	**1,003**	1.9%
Commitments and contingencies (Notes 23&29)				
Total liabilities	**13,756**	21.8%	**11,391**	21.5%
Stockholders' equity:				
Preferred stock, $0.001 par value, 50 shares authorized; none issued	—		—	
Common stock, $0.001 par value, 10,000 shares authorized; 5,581 issued and 5,511				
outstanding (5,523 issued and outstanding in 2009) and capital in excess of par value	16,178	25.6%	14,993	28.2%
Accumulated other comprehensive income (loss)	333	0.5%	393	0.7%
Retained earnings	32,919	52.1%	26,318	49.6%
Total stockholders' equity	**49,430**	78.2%	**41,704**	78.5%
Total liabilities and stockholders' equity	**63,186**	100.0%	**53,095**	100.0%

The common size balance sheet for Intel Corporation reveals the following:

1. Total current assets are a greater percent of total assets in 2010 than in 2009 due to an increase of approximately $8 billion (57%) in cash and cash equivalents, short-term investments, and trading assets.

2. Accounts receivable and inventory increased slightly as a percent of total assets. The turnover ratios for accounts receivable and inventory (discussed later in this chapter) should be used to determine if the increase in each asset is proportionate to the increase sales.

3. Property, plant and equipment, net has decreased as a percent of total assets; however, the total amount has increased. The percent decrease is due to the increase in cash and investments which caused the majority of the increase in total assets.

4. Marketable securities and other long-term investments have decreased. Some long-term investments may have moved to cash equivalents or short-term investments.

5. Total current liabilities as a percent of total assets have not changed significantly from one year to the next. Long-term debt is a lower percentage compared to total assets due to the increase in total assets. The total amount of long-term debt has not changed significantly.

Example 10-2 continued:

6. Total stockholders' equity has not changed significantly as a percent of total assets. Common stock and capital is a lower percentage even though the amount increased because of the increase in total assets. The increase in retained earnings is primarily the result of earnings kept for reinvestment in the company.

7. The increase in total assets is a result of the increase in common stock and capital and earned income in retained earnings that flowed through to cash and investments. The company did not invest in significant additional long-term assets to use in the business.

Financial Ratio Analysis

Relationships between financial statement amounts are referred to as financial ratios. Financial ratio analysis is used to compare companies of different sizes. Investors and creditors use ratio analysis to determine future earnings and estimate the ability to repay debt. Management uses ratio analysis to help them make operating and capital investment decisions.

Many different financial statement ratios are used to discover strengths and weaknesses of a company. This chapter will discuss some of the most common ratios used by investors and creditors.

Ratios that use information from the income statement and the balance sheet are computed using an average amount for the balance sheet item. The income statement amount occurred during the entire year. A balance sheet amount that represents the average for the year is more comparable to the income statement annual amount than using a beginning or an ending amount.

> The average amount is computed as: (Current Year + Prior Year) / 2

The following pages present financial ratios of four companies in two different industries. The ratios are computed using information provided on the financial statements for the year ending as noted below for the following companies:

> The Home Depot, Inc. and subsidiaries (HD) as of and year ended January 28, 2012
> The Lowe's Companies, Inc. (Lowe's) as of and year ended February 2, 2012
> Apple, Inc. as of and year ended September 23, 2011
> Google Inc. as of and year ended December 31, 2011

Balance Sheet Ratios

Debt to Equity $=$ $\dfrac{\text{Total Liabilities}}{\text{Total Stockholders' Equity}}$

**Long-term
Debt to Equity** $=$ $\dfrac{\text{Total Long-term Liabilities}}{\text{Total Stockholders' Equity}}$

The debt to equity and the long-term debt to equity ratios indicate how a company finances growth. A ratio higher than 1.0 indicates that more funds have been raised through debt than from owners and retained earnings. Funds obtained from owners do not have to be repaid. Funds from borrowing must be repaid with interest. A high level of debt may be positive if the company is able to earn more than the interest cost on the debt. A high level of debt can be very negative if the company does not have enough liquidity to repay debt when it becomes due. It is important to determine the different types of long-term liabilities a company has and when long-term liabilities are expected to be repaid. Debt to equity ratios are not used to determine the ability to repay liabilities.

	HD	Lowe's	Apple	Google
Total Liabilities	22,620	17,026	39,756	14,429
Total Stockholders' Equity	17,898	16,533	76,615	58,145
Ratio	126%	103%	52%	25%

	HD	Lowe's	Apple	Google
Total Long-term Liabilities	13,244	9,135	11,786	5,516
Total Stockholders' Equity	17,898	16,533	76,615	58,145
Ratio	74.0%	55.3%	15.4%	9.5%

Comparing Home Depot and Lowe's:

Both Home Depot and Lowe's have purchased fewer assets with debt than with funds obtained from owners and reinvested profits. Home Depot relies more on long-term debt than Lowe's. Relying more on debt often leads to a higher return on equity when the company earns more than the interest cost of borrowing.

Comparing Apple and Google:

The majority of total liabilities for both companies is current liabilities. Google has less long-term liabilities; however, both have very low ratios and the difference in the two companies is not significant. Both companies have primarily financed growth using funds from owners and earnings.

Current Ratio = $\dfrac{\text{Current Assets}}{\text{Current Liabilities}}$

Quick Ratio = $\dfrac{\text{Liquid Current Assets}}{\text{Current Liabilities}}$

The current ratio and the quick ratio (also called the acid test) indicate the company's ability to pay operating expenses. Liquid current assets are expected to be cash within the time accounts payable and other current liabilities are due to be paid; generally 30 days. Liquid current assets include cash and cash equivalents, short-term investments, and accounts receivable. The quick ratio indicates if cash is expected to be available to pay current liabilities. Both ratios exclude long-term investments that may be available to sell if necessary to generate cash because the company does not <u>intend</u> to sell the investments in time to pay current liabilities.

A current or quick ratio of 1.0 or better indicates the company has resources available to pay current liabilities.

	HD	**Lowe's**	**Apple**	**Google**
Current Assets	14,520	10,072	44,988	52,758
Current Liabilities	9,376	7,891	27,970	8,913
Ratio	1.55	1.28	1.61	5.92

	HD	**Lowe's**	**Apple**	**Google**
Liquid Current Assets	3,232	1,300	37,669	50,798
Current Liabilities	9,376	7,891	27,970	8,913
Ratio	0.35	0.17	1.35	5.70

Comparing Home Depot to Lowe's:

Both appear to have enough total current assets and not near enough liquid assets to pay current liabilities over the next year. The primary difference in current assets and liquid assets for both companies is significant amounts of inventory.

Both companies must sell inventory and collect from customers timely in order to be able to pay current liabilities. Home Depot does not have current notes payable or long-term investments. Lowe's has about $500 million in long-term investments that could be sold to repay about $500 million of current maturities of long-term debt.

The current and quick ratios for the past few years should be computed to determine if the situation is deteriorating or if this is generally the way the home improvement retail industry operates. It appears as if neither company will be able to pay current liabilities; however, both companies have been operating with very limited liquidity for the past few years.

116

Comparing Apple to Google:

Almost all of Google's current assets are liquid due to the fact that they do not have inventory. Apple manages their inventory very efficiently (see inventory turnover ratio). A closer look at the balance sheets of each reveals that Google has minimal long-term investments (790 million) and Apple has a significant amount of long-term investments ($55.6 billion). The current ratio for Apple would be 3.60 and the quick ratio would be 3.09 if long-term investments were classified as short-term investments. Both companies appear to have the ability to easily pay current liabilities.

Total Liabilities to Total Assets = $\dfrac{\text{Total Liabilities}}{\text{Total Assets}}$

This ratio indicates how much of the cost of the company's assets have not yet been paid. All assets are either not yet paid (a liability) or paid (stockholders equity.)

	HD	**Lowe's**	**Apple**	**Google**
Total Liabilities	22,620	17,026	39,756	14,429
Total Assets	40,578	33,559	116,371	72,574
Ratio	55.8%	50.7%	34.2%	19.9%

Comparing Home Depot to Lowe's:

Both companies own approximately half of their assets. The ratios indicate no significant difference in how the two companies finance the purchase of assets.

Comparing Apple to Google:

Apple owns a larger percent of their assets than Google. A closer look at the balance sheet reveals that Apple has $10,100 of other long-term liabilities consisting of mostly deferred taxes that will be paid in the future. The large amount of deferred taxes (not debt) causes the ratio to be higher for Apple than Google. Google has $3,000 of long-term debt and $1,235 owed for income taxes. Apple and Google both have enough cash and cash equivalents and investments to immediately pay all liabilities and have cash left to operate the business.

A high amount of liabilities is generally not viewed negatively as long as the borrowed funds generate more than the cost of the debt and the amounts owed do not become so high that it is difficult for the company to repay the debt using cash generated from operations.

Inventory Turnover = $\dfrac{\text{Cost of Goods Sold}}{\text{Average Inventory}}$

and then $\dfrac{365 \text{ days}}{\text{Inventory turnover}}$

This ratio indicates how many days on average inventory is in the warehouse before it is sold.

	HD	Lowe's	Apple	Google
Cost of Goods Sold	46,133	32,858	64,431	13,188
Average Inventory	10,475	8,988	914	0
= Inventory Turnover	4.40	3.66	70.5	0
$\dfrac{365 \text{ Days}}{\text{Inventory Turnover}}$	$\dfrac{365}{4.40}$	$\dfrac{365}{3.66}$	$\dfrac{365}{70.5}$	$\dfrac{365}{0}$
Days in the Warehouse	83.0	99.7	5.2	0

Slow moving inventory uses cash and can indicate sales are slowing. This ratio should be done for the past two to three years to determine trends.

Comparing Home Depot to Lowe's:

Both are retail companies that have to balance having too much inventory with not enough inventory to satisfy customer desires. Home Depot appears to manage this delicate balance slightly better. The ability to predict customer buying patterns allows a company to minimize the amount of inventory necessary to service customers.

Comparing Apple to Google:

Google is a service company and does not sell inventory. Apple sold products that were in high demand and had trouble producing enough to meet demand in 2011. Apple also sells direct to other retailers which reduces the amount of inventory that Apple has to store in its warehouse.

Accounts Receivable Turnover = $$\frac{\text{Total Sales}}{\text{Average Accounts Receivables}}$$

and then $$\frac{\text{365 days}}{\text{Accounts Receivable Turnover}}$$

Total sales is often referred to as total revenues or net sales. Assume all sales reported on the income statement are credit sales unless otherwise stated.

This ratio indicates how many days it normally takes to collect from customers after the goods or services are provided. Slow collection could lead to increased bad debt expense and the inability to pay day to day operating expenses. Days to collect that creeps higher each year often indicates growing uncollectible accounts.

	HD	Lowe's	Apple	Google
Total Sales	70,395	50,208	108,249	37,905
Average Accounts Receivable	1,165	0	10,821	4,840
= Accounts Receivable Turnover	60.4	0	10.0	7.8
365 Days	365	365	365	365
A/R Turnover	60.4	0	10.0	7.8
Days to Collect	6.0	0	36.5	46.8

Comparing Home Depot to Lowe's:

Lowe's sells all receivables to third parties. Home Depot accepts credit cards which pay within 2-5 days and extends minimal credit to contractors. The weak quick ratios of both companies indicate neither can afford to wait many days to collect cash from customers.

Comparing Apple to Google:

Apple collects about 10 days sooner from customers than Google. Apple can ask for and enforce quicker payment because products are in high demand. Domestic customers for both companies are generally extended 30 day terms. Both companies do significant business with international customers who often get extended terms of up to 90 days.

Sales to Total Assets = $\dfrac{\text{Sales}}{\text{Average Total Assets}}$

Sales to Total Fixed Assets = $\dfrac{\text{Sales}}{\text{Average Total Fixed Assets*}}$

* Fixed Assets is another term for property, plant, and equipment.

These ratios indicate how efficiently assets are used to generate sales.

	HD	Lowe's	Apple	Google
$\dfrac{\text{Sales}}{\text{Average Total Assets}}$	$\dfrac{70,395}{40,322}$	$\dfrac{50,208}{33,629}$	$\dfrac{108,249}{95,777}$	$\dfrac{37,905}{65,213}$
Ratio	1.75	1.49	1.13	0.58

	HD	Lowe's	Apple	Google
$\dfrac{\text{Sales}}{\text{Average Total Fixed Assets}}$	$\dfrac{70,395}{24,754}$	$\dfrac{50,208}{22,030}$	$\dfrac{108,249}{6,273}$	$\dfrac{37,905}{8,681}$
Ratio	2.84	2.28	17.26	4.37

Comparing Home Depot to Lowe's:

The difference in total assets and fixed assets for both companies is primarily inventory and some cash. Home Depot generates more sales with less fixed assets and lower levels of inventory. Generating more sales on fewer assets produces a higher return on assets.

Comparing Apple to Google:

Apple generates a much higher amount of sales from each dollar invested in assets than Google. Apple has manufacturing facilities. Google has server facilities. The investment in fixed assets is relatively small compared to total assets for both companies due to large amounts of cash and investments.

Profitability Ratios

Gross Profit Margin   =   Gross Profit
$$\frac{\text{Gross Profit}}{\text{Sales}}$$

	HD	Lowe's	Apple	Google
Gross Profit	24,262	17,350	43,818	24,717
Sales	70,395	50,208	108,249	37,905
Ratio	34.5%	34.6%	40.5%	65.2%

Comparing Home Depot to Lowe's:

Both companies sell the same types of products in a very price competitive environment. Neither company appears to have an advantage when it comes to pricing products.

Comparing Apple to Google:

Google's gross profit is calculated after subtracting direct costs of providing services since no products are sold. Apple has more competitors than Google, which restricts pricing options. Google earns more from each sales dollar than Apple. Given the same growth in sales dollars, Google would be expected to increase profits at a faster rate than Apple.

Operating Profit Margin   =   Operating Income
$$\frac{\text{Operating Income}}{\text{Sales}}$$

	HD	Lowe's	Apple	Google
Operating Income	6,661	3,277	33,790	11,742
Sales	70,395	50,208	108,249	37,905
Ratio	9.5%	6.5%	31.2%	31.0%

Comparing Home Depot to Lowe's:

The income statements indicate that Home Depot operates the business with lower selling and administrative expenses than Lowe's. This gives Home Depot higher operating income than Lowe's. Home Depot generates $0.03 more in operating income for each sales dollar than Lowes.

Comparing Apple to Google:

There is very little difference in Apple and Google. A dollar increase in sales should generate about $0.31 of operating profit. The company that grows sales dollars at the fastest rate will increase operating income at a faster rate.

Profit Margin   = $\dfrac{\text{Net Income}}{\text{Sales}}$

The profit margin ratio indicates the portion of each sales dollar that becomes net income.

	HD	**Lowe's**	**Apple**	**Google**
Net Income	3.883	1,839	25,922	9,737
Sales	70,395	50,208	108,249	37,905
Ratio	5.5%	3.7%	24.0%	25.7%

Comparing Home Depot to Lowe's:

Home Depot generates more net income per sales dollar due to lower operating expenses.

Comparing Apple to Google:

Apple and Google are about the same, which is to be expected when the operating ratio is about the same. Approximately one quarter of each sales dollar becomes net income. The ability to generate high levels of earnings strengthens all other ratios.

Return on Assets   = $\dfrac{\text{Net Income}}{\text{Average Total Assets}}$

or

$$\dfrac{\text{Income before Interest and Tax}}{\text{Average Total Assets}}$$

Return on assets indicates the percent return on each dollar that is invested in assets.

	HD	**Lowe's**	**Apple**	**Google**
Net Income	3,883	1,839	25,922	9,737
Average Total Assets	40,322	33,629	95,777	65,213
Ratio	9.6%	5.5%	27.1%	14.9%

	HD	Lowe's	Apple	Google
Income Before Interest and Tax	6,674	3,277	34,205	12,326
Average Total Assets	40,322	33,629	95,777	65,213
Ratio	16.6%	9.8%	35.7%	18.9%

Comparing Home Depot to Lowe's:

Home Depot generates more income from their investments in assets than Lowe's. This is a result of higher sales generated from assets and lower operating expenses.

Comparing Apple to Google:

Apple generates a higher return on assets used to operate the business than Google. Both companies have almost no interest expense. The difference in the two ratios is due to income tax expense. The ratios for both companies are lower due to the significant amount of cash and investments. Cash and investments earned much less than operating the business during 2011.

Return on Equity = $\dfrac{\text{Net Income}}{\text{Average Stockholders' Equity}}$

Return on equity indicates the percent return on each dollar that remains invested by the owners.

	HD	Lowe's	Apple	Google
Net Income	3,883	1,839	25,922	9,737
Average Stockholder's Equity	18,394	17,323	62,203	52,193
Ratio	21.1%	10.6%	41.7%	18.7%

All four companies provide a strong return on investment compared to other investments available in 2011. The risk free rate of return on United States treasury bonds in 2011 was approximately two to three percent.

Comparing Home Depot to Lowe's:

Home Depot equity owners are earning a higher return on their investment in the company. Home Depot's return is higher than Lowe's due to lower operating expenses. Home Depot's operating margin ratio is higher than its current cost of debt. The use of debt leads to a higher return on equity when the borrowed funds earn more than the cost of interest. Home Depot also has a higher debt to equity ratio than Lowes.

Comparing Apple to Google:

Apple has a higher return on equity than Google. Neither company has financed operations with long-term debt or has paid dividends to common stockholders.

Investor Ratios

Earnings per Share *** $=$ $$\frac{\text{Net Income} - \text{Preferred Dividends}}{\text{Average Number of Common Shares Outstanding}}$$

Price to Earnings $=$ $$\frac{\text{Fair Market Value of One Common Share}}{\text{Earnings per Share}}$$

	HD	Lowe's	Apple	Google
Market Value of one Share on December 31, 2011**	$42	$25	$404	$646
Basic Earnings per Share***	$2.49	$1.43	$28.05	$30.17
= Price to Earnings	16.9	17.5	14.4	21.4

** The market value of one share is not stated in the financial statements. Market value on a specific date is provided by the stock exchange and can easily be found on a financial website such as www.yahoo.finance.com

*** Basic Earnings per Share is provided by the company on the bottom of the income statement.

Earnings per share represent the current earnings for one share of common stock.

The price to earnings ratio indicates investors' expectations of the long-term annual rate of growth of the company. A higher price to earnings ratios indicates investors expect a higher rate of growth.

The earnings per share ratio is used by investors to determine the approximate fair market value per share on December 31, 2011:

	HD	Lowe's	Apple	Google
Earnings per share	$2.49	$1.43	$28.05	$30.17
x **Annual expected growth %**	**16.9%**	**17.5%**	**14.4%**	**21.4%**
= Fair market value of one share of common stock	$ 42	$ 25	$ 404	$ 646

Actual earnings growth from:

	HD	Lowe's	Apple	Google
2009 to 2010	25%	13%	70%	30%
2010 to 2011	16%	9%	113%	15%

Actual earnings growth is computed as the current year earnings per share less the prior year earnings per share divided by the prior year earnings per share.

Comparing Home Depot to Lowe's:

Investors are expecting similar growth from Home Depot and Lowe's and do not perceive that one company has a significant advantage over the other. The expectation for future growth for Lowe's is not supported by the actual growth trends. Home Depot has grown at a faster rate in prior years than Lowe's; a trend that may or may not continue.

Comparing Apple to Google:

Investors are expecting stronger consistent growth from Google. Investors do not expect Apple to be able to continue the current rate of significant growth over a long period of time.
See chapter 5 for further discussion of earning per share.

Financial statement analysis using ratios allows the user of the financial statements to view the company from many different perspectives when making a decision to invest or lend. It allows the user of financial statements to see the relationships between the balance sheet and the income statement. Financial statement ratio analysis does not provide a "right answer"; ratios are tools to use along with strong business judgment when making financial decisions.

11. Accounting Estimates and Other Things to Consider

The language of accounting must be understood in order to read financial statements and footnotes. The following items must also be considered when using financial information:

1) Accountants **estimate** many amounts that are reported on the financial statements. All reported amounts have not actually occurred.

2) The change in cash and cash equivalents reported on the cash flow statement does not represent the performance of the company for the period.

3) Most amounts on the balance sheet are stated at historical cost. A balance sheet does not report the total fair market value of a company.

Estimates

The accrual basis of accounting requires that all expenses incurred to generate revenue during the period must be reported in the same period. It is common for the accountant to know from past experience that an expense associated with sales will occur and not know the exact amount because the exchange has not happened yet. It is also possible for the accountant to estimate that assets have lost value and not be able to determine the exact amount of the loss until a later period. Accountants estimate amounts using past experience as a guide for future expectations.

All estimates made in the current period are estimated again in the next period. When an estimate differs from the actual amount, the company does NOT go back and change the prior period financial statement to the actual amount. Inaccurate (wrong) estimates are corrected on future period financial statements.   Estimates that are too high (or too low) in the current period are adjusted lower (or higher) in future periods. Accounts that are commonly affected by estimates are discussed below.

Accounts receivable, net is an estimated amount. Accounts receivable is an asset. The value reported for an asset cannot be higher than the expected probable future economic benefit from the asset. Companies know from past experience that customers will not pay certain amounts due to 1) customer returns, 2) customer rebates, 3) early payment discounts, 4) volume discounts after a certain volume is reached, 5) customer disputes regarding amounts owed, and 6) customer bankruptcies.

The company does not know the exact amount that will not be received in future periods. Total accounts receivable is reduced by the amount not expected to be collected. The net amount reported on the balance sheet is the amount expected to be collected (the expected probable future economic benefit.)

The estimate of amounts not expected to be collected are recorded by accountants using a contra asset account named "allowance for…" The receivable is recorded at the total amount owed by the customer and the allowance account is netted against the receivable account.

The reduction to the amount of accounts receivable reported on the balance sheet is also either a reduction to **sales** or an increase to an **operating expense** on the income statement as follows:

Balance Sheet   Income Statement

Balance Sheet	Income Statement
Accounts receivable	**Sales**
- Allowance for returns	- Sales returns
- Allowance for rebates	- Sales rebates
- Allowance for payment discounts	- Sales discounts
- Allowance for volume discounts	- Volume discounts
- Allowance for uncollectible accounts	= **Net Sales**
= **Accounts Receivable, Net**	
	Operating Expenses:
	- Bad debt expense

Accounts receivable and sales are stated at the initial value provided to customers; an agreed upon price that is not an estimated amount. All other items listed as reductions to accounts receivable and sales are estimates made by the accountant because the company expects (based on past history) that customers will not pay these amounts.

Most deductions from accounts receivable are estimated based on a historical percent of sales for the period.

Inventory is initially reported at historical cost and then reviewed to determine if it has lost value. Lost value generally occurs when competitors sell the same type of products at lower prices or when new products become available. It is better to sell the inventory for less than cost than to not sell it at all. This is particularly common with clothing and technology.

A company must reduce the amount for inventory reported on the balance sheet to the expected net sales price (net realizable value) when they suspect it will be sold at a loss. A company cannot wait until inventory is actually sold for less than cost to report a loss. Inventory cannot be reported on the balance sheet at a value higher than the expected probable future economic benefit (net sales price.) The accountant must estimate the loss in value in the period the inventory loses value. An additional cost of goods sold expense is reported on the income statement during the period the inventory loses value.

Example 11-1 illustrates very simply how lost value is determined. The company has two products in inventory with an expected sales price and historical cost as follows:

	Product 1	Product 2	Total If Grouped
Current net sales price	$10	$ 10	$20
- Historical Cost	($ 8)	($15)	($23)
= Lost value (if negative)	$ 2	($ 5)	($ 3)

Product 1 will be reported on the balance sheet at the historical cost of $8; an amount lower than the net sales price. No adjustment is made to increase the value above original cost. Product 2 will be reported on the balance sheet at the net sales price of $10 because it is lower than historical cost. Inventory cannot be reported at higher than the net sales price.

The balance sheet and income statement will report the following given there were only two products held in inventory.

Balance Sheet:	Income Statement:
Inventory $18	Cost of Goods Sold ($5)

GAAP allows a company to group similar products when determining if inventory has lost value. Inventory would be reported at $20 and cost of goods sold would be reported at $3 if the company chose to evaluate inventory in total.

Inventory is often purchased at different costs at different times or from different suppliers. The company does not know the actual cost of items remaining in the warehouse or the cost of specific items sold when all items look the same and cost different amounts.

Accountants must chose a method of accounting that estimates which cost was sold and which cost remains in the warehouse. Three acceptable methods under GAAP used to value inventory are referred to as: 1) last in first out (LIFO), 2) first in first out (FIFO), and 3) average cost. Each method gives a different <u>estimated</u> cost of inventory and cost of goods sold reported on the financial statements.

Example 11-2 illustrates the difference in the three acceptable methods used to value inventory and cost of goods sold.

	Quantity	x	Cost for 1	=	Total Cost	
1/1	100	x	$23	=	$ 2,300	
1/8	350	x	$24	=	$ 8,400	
1/12	200	x	$25	=	$ 5,000	
1/22	100	x	$26	=	$ 2,600	
	750	Total Available			$ 18,300	
	(330)	Total Sold			$????	cannot tell by looking; different costs
	420	End of Period Inventory			$????	cannot tell by looking; different costs

129

Example 11-2 continued

FIFO (first in first out): Assumes items **purchased first** are **sold first**.

Sold

1/1	100	x	$23	=	$2,300	
1/8	230	x	$24	=	$5,520	
	330				$7,820	Cost of Goods Sold

Total Available	$18,300	
- Cost of Goods Sold	$ 7,820	reported on the income statement
= Inventory	$10,480	reported on the balance sheet

The last items purchased are assumed to remain in inventory.

LIFO (last in first out): Assumes items **purchased last** are **sold first**.

Sold

1/22	100	x	$26	=	$2,600	
1/12	200	x	$25	=	$5,000	
1/8	30	x	$24	=	$ 720	
	330				$8,320	Cost of Goods Sold

Total Available	$18,300	
- Cost of Goods Sold	$ 8,320	reported on the income statement
= Inventory	$ 9,980	reported on the balance sheet

The first items purchased are assumed to remain in inventory.

Weighted Average: Inventory is valued at the average purchase cost.

$$\frac{\text{Total Available Cost}}{\text{Total Available Quantity}} = \frac{\$18,300}{750} = \$24.40 \text{ average cost per item}$$

$24.40 average cost per item x 330 units sold = $8,052 cost of goods sold

Total Available	$18,300	
- Cost of Goods Sold	$ 8,052	reported on the income statement
= Inventory	$10,248	reported on the balance sheet

Each method results in a different value of inventory and cost of goods sold reported on the financial statements. The accountant estimates the reported amounts based on the method selected because **the actual correct amount is not known.**

130

Property, plant, and equipment is reported on the balance sheet **"net"** of the cost of using the assets for all periods the assets have been used. The company does not know the exact cost of using each long-term asset each period. The cost for each period is estimated and reported as depreciation expense. There are several different methods that can be used to estimated depreciation. One method, called straight-line, estimates the same expense for each period. Another method, called double-declining balance, estimate a higher cost in earlier years and lower cost in later years. Another method, called units of production, estimates the cost based on the quantity of product produced. Each acceptable method gives a different estimated expense and net value reported on the financial statements.

A key factor used in estimating depreciation expense is how many years the company expects to use the asset to produce revenue. Spreading the cost over more years reduces the expense for each year and spreading the cost over fewer years increases the expense for each year. Companies normally decide on a standard length of time for each type of asset category. The estimated number of years assets are expected to be used is disclosed in the footnotes.

The estimate impacts the net asset amount reported on the balance sheet and the depreciation expense reported on the income statement as follows.

Balance Sheet:	Income Statement:
Property, Plant and Equipment - Accumulated Depreciation = Property, Plant and Equipment, **Net**	Depreciation Expense

Property, plant, and equipment, net and depreciation expense are both estimated amounts.

Intangible assets are reported on the balance sheet **"net"** of the cost of using the assets for all periods the assets have been used. The cost of using each intangible asset each period, reported as amortization expense, is not known and must be estimated. Most companies spread the cost equally over each year the asset is used (the straight-line method.) Intangible assets, net and amortization expense are both estimated amounts because the useful life is estimated. Estimated amounts are reported on the financial statements as follows:

Balance Sheet:	Income Statement:
Intangible assets - Accumulated Depreciation = Intangible assets, **Net**	Amortization Expense

A **warranty** is a promise made by a company to replace defective goods or refund cash if the product does not perform as expected. A company does not know the cost of customers that will request a replacement or refund at the time the sale is made. The amount of the future cost must be estimated and reported as warranty expense in the same period as the sale. Warranty costs in prior periods are used to predict what might occur in future periods. The cost of offering the warranty is reported on the financial statements at the estimated amount as follows:

Balance Sheet:	Income Statement:
Warranty Liability	Warranty Expense

Loss contingencies are amounts that may have to be paid because a certain event has occurred. The amount that will be paid in future periods is uncertain at the time the financial statements are provided. The most common loss contingencies are lawsuits and environment cleanups.

GAAP requires the company to report the contingency on the financial statements based on one of three categories. The category is determined by management and the situation is reported for each category as follows:

Category	Required Reporting
Probable	Report a loss on the income statement and liability on the balance sheet for the estimated amount. Describe the situation in the footnotes.
Reasonably Possible	Describe the situation in the footnotes. Nothing reported on the financial statements.
Remote	Nothing is reported on the financial statement or in the footnotes.

A **probable loss** contingency is reported on the financial statements for the low end of the estimated amount as follows:

Balance Sheet:	Income Statement:
Contingent Liability	Loss Contingency

Most contingencies are categorized as "reasonably possibly" and no loss is reported on the income statement until the amount to be paid becomes fairly certain. The estimated range of loss is disclosed in the footnotes.

Income tax expense is initially recorded as a percent of income before taxes. The percent is determined by the government where the company does business. Income tax rules are often open to the interpretation and a company's tax accountant. The company's tax accountant's interpretation is subject to the judgment of the Internal Revenue Service (IRS) agent who audits the company. Companies will often record additional income tax expense just in case the IRS agent disagrees with the amount of taxable income reported on the tax return. The additional income tax expense is an estimate.

The estimate of what might have to be paid in the future impacts the income tax liability reported on the balance sheet and the income tax expense reported on the income statement.

<table>
<tr><td>Balance Sheet:</td><td>Income Statement:</td></tr>
<tr><td>Income Tax Payable
  (or Deferred Tax Liability)</td><td>Income Tax Expense</td></tr>
</table>

Goodwill that occurs when a company purchases another company is also an estimated amount. Goodwill is computed as follows:

   The amount paid to purchase the entire company
- The fair market value of the net identifiable assets and liabilities of the company purchased
= Goodwill reported on the balance sheet.

Judgment is often required to determine the fair market value of the identified assets and liabilities.

Goodwill is an estimated amount because the fair market value of identified assets and liabilities purchased is an estimate. A company is likely to allocate as much value as possible to goodwill because goodwill is not expensed each period like other long-term assets with a limited useful life. See chapter 2 for further discussion of goodwill.

The line items on the income statement that contain estimates are as follows:

Sales, Net	Estimated
- Cost of Goods Sold	Estimated (inventory)
= Gross Profit	Estimated
- Operating Expenses	Estimated (depreciation, amortization, warranty, bad debt, etc.)
= Operating Income	
+- Other Revenues and Expenses	Estimated (loss contingencies and gain or loss on asset sales)
= Income Before Taxes:	
- Income Tax Expense	Estimated (audit risk)
= Net Income	**Estimated!**

The following assets and liabilities are reported on the balance sheet at estimated amounts:

Accounts receivable, net	Warranty liabilities
Inventory, net	Income tax payable
Property, plant, and equipment, Net	Deferred income tax
Intangible assets, Net	Loss contingencies
Goodwill	

The word "NET" on financial statements generally indicates the value reported has been reduced by an estimated amount.

All estimates for the current period are estimated again in the following periods. When an estimated amount is not equal to the actual amount, the company does NOT go back and change the prior period financial statement to the actual amount.

Example 11-3 illustrates how changes in bad debt expense estimates are reported. The estimated amount is $10,000 in the current period. The estimate is revised to $12,000 in the next period and $9,000 in the following period. The estimate is reported on the income statement as follows:

	Current Period	Next Period	Following Period
Bad Debt Expense	$10,000	$2,000	($3,000)
	lower income	lower income	higher income

The difference in each estimate is reported in the period the estimate is changed.

The Cash Flow Statement

The fact that the income statement contains many estimates leads some users of financial statements to believe that net income is often manipulated to achieve desired results. The reliability of financial information is dependent on sound ethical judgment of accountants. Accountants must ensure that the methods used and the estimated amounts represent the economic results of the business and do not mislead users.

Some users of financial statements rely heavily on the cash flow statement because they believe the cash flow statement cannot be manipulated. They believe that cash is a black and white number and an increase in cash means the company has real earnings and economic gains.

Those who believe the cash flow statement cannot be manipulated have forgotten that the cash flow statement reports transactions that occur <u>during a period of time.</u> Transactions that impact cash can be expedited or delayed. Cash can be obtained from sources other than earnings. The cash balance at the end of a given period of time can be manipulated.

Ways a company can intentionally increase the net change in cash reported on the cash flow statement are listed below:

1) Offer customers a discount for early payment. This is a cost to the company that reduces earnings; however, cash will be collected sooner from most customers who are offered a discount.

2) Delay payment of accounts payable and accrued liabilities a few days until the next period.

3) Delay purchases of inventory until the next period.

4) Sell investments and do not reinvest the cash until the next period.

5) Delay purchases of property and equipment until the next period.

6) Borrow money and increase cash in bank accounts.

7) Pay less dividends to stockholders or delay the payment date until the next period.

8) Cancel or delay treasury stock purchases.

9) Delay expansion projects or acquisitions of other companies until future periods.

A company can intentionally decrease the amount of cash on hand by doing the opposite of the above. It is very important that the cash flow statement be analyzed to determine what types of transactions caused an increase or decrease in cash. An increase in cash is not always a sign that the company is improving its financial position. See chapter 8 for further discussion of the cash flow statement.

The Fair Market Value of a Company

The balance sheet is the statement of financial position of the company. This financial statement details the items a company owns or controls and uses to operate the business (assets) and amounts owed to others (liabilities.)

Almost all amounts reported on the balance sheet are stated **at historical cost**. Amounts are reported at historical **cost** because historical cost is **reliable** and can be **verified.** See chapter 2 for further discussion.

A significant limitation of reporting values at historical cost is the amounts **most likely do not represent current fair market value.**

Historical cost is the amount <u>paid</u> for an asset.

Fair market value is the amount an asset could be <u>sold for or the total future cash flows</u> an asset is expected to generate.

A significant difference between the historical cost reported on the balance sheet and the estimated fair market value of assets may exist. The following must be considered when reading the balance sheet:

1) The value of an asset cannot be reported at an amount that is higher than the expected probable future economic benefit (future cash flows) of using the asset. When future cash flows are expected to be lower than historical cost, the amount on the balance sheet must be reduced to the value of expected probable future cash flows. A permanent reduction from cost to fair market value is called **impairment.**

Assets are not reported at an amount higher than historical cost. The gain from an increase in fair market value of long-term assets is not reported on the financial statements until the period the asset is actually sold. (This may be different for investments, see next page.)

2) Property, plant, and equipment is reported at book value. Book value is equal to historical cost less accumulated depreciation. Book value is the amount that will be expensed over future periods. Assets generally lose fair market value at different rates than the expense is reported on the income statement. Book value is not an attempt to estimate fair market value in any way.

3) Intangible assets are reported at the amount paid to those <u>outside</u> the company less the cost of using the assets in all prior periods (net book value.) Costs incurred internally to develop intangible assets are expensed when incurred and are not reported on the balance sheet. The book value for intangible assets is often minimal compared to the asset's ability to generate future cash flows.

136

4) Investments made for appreciation and income that have a <u>reliable fair market value</u> are reported at fair market value on the balance sheet. A reliable fair market value is one that is quoted on a stock exchange in the case of equity investments or has a very stable cash flow associated with the investment in a debt. Investments without a reliable fair market value are reported at cost.

5) Internally generated goodwill is not reported on the balance sheet. This consists of a good management team, strong customer relationships, good locations, customer lists, and a good brand name; among other things. Internally generated goodwill often has a very high fair market value because it includes expected future earnings. The future cash flows expected to be generated by the business is not reported on the balance sheet unless it is purchased goodwill.

Example 11-4 presents the balance sheets for Sears Holding Company. The balance sheet reports values at historical cost or book value. A discussion of the differences between amounts reported on the balance sheet at historical cost or book value and the total fair market value of Sears Holding Company follows:

1) Merchandise inventories are stated at historical cost. The amount of $8,407 does not represent the net cash expected to be received from selling the products to customers.

2) Accounts receivable, net of 695 is an estimated amount of what is expected to be collected from customers. The amount that is expected to be uncollectible is not large enough to state.

3) Property, plant, and equipment, net is reported at historical cost less estimated accumulated depreciation. The amount of $6,577 is the amount that has not yet been expensed. This amount does not represent the fair market value of the assets (expected current sales price or future cash flow generated from using the assets.)

4) Goodwill, and trade names and other intangible assets, net is reported at the amount paid to purchase the asset less any amortization expense for those with a defined useful life. The amount does not represent fair market value (current sales price or expected future cash flows generated from using the assets.)

5) Liabilities are reported at the unpaid principle amount on the balance sheet date.

6) Common stock and capital represents the amount that was initially contributed to the company for ownership. It does not represent the current fair market value of the stock.

7) The ability to generate ongoing profits from the business (internally generated goodwill) is not reported on the balance sheet.

Example 11-4 continued:

As of January, 28, 2012, Sears Holding Company had a total fair market value as follows:

	Fair market value for one share of common stock	$44
x	Approximate number of outstanding common shares	106,000,000
=	Total fair market value of the entire company	$4,664,000,000

The fair market value that is not reported on the balance sheet is computed as follows:

	Total fair market value of the company	$4,664,000,000
-	Total book value (equity) of the company	($4,341,000,000)
=	Fair market value not reported on the balance sheet	$ 323,000,000

The company generated operating losses in 2012 (see the income statement) and the total fair market value for the company takes this into consideration. A fair market value slightly higher than book value indicates that assets are not expected to generate much more future cash flow than the reported book value (total stockholders' equity.)

Investors expect Sears Holding Company to earn a loss per share for 2013 of approximately $4.00 per share, a total loss of approximately $400 million for the company.

If losses continue, the management team at Sears Holding Company will have to determine whether additional loss on impairment of long-term assets has occurred. Continued losses indicate long-term assets are losing their ability to generate positive future cash flows. Goodwill is lower in 2012 than 2011. The income statement reports a loss on impairment of $649 for the year ended 2012.

Sears Holding Company
Consolidated Balance Sheet

	January 28, 2012	January 29, 2011
Cash and cash equivalents	747	1,359
Restricted cash	7	15
Accounts receivable, net	695	689
Merchandise inventories	8,407	8,951
Prepaid expenses and other current assets	388	334
Current assets of discontinued operations	0	212
Total current assets	10,244	11,560

Example 11-4: Sears Holding Company Consolidated Balance Sheet (continued)

	January 28, 2012	January 29, 2011
Property and equipment	11,210	11,329
less accumulated depreciation	(4,633)	(4,227)
Total property and equipment, net	6,577	7,102
Goodwill	841	1,392
Trade names and other intangibles, net	2,937	2,993
Other assets	782	899
Noncurrent assets of discontinued operations	0	414
Total assets	21,381	24,360
Short-term borrowings	1,175	360
Current portion of long-term debt and		
capital lease obligations	230	489
Merchandise payables	2,912	3,046
Other current liabilities	2,892	2,937
Unearned revenues	964	976
Other taxes	523	546
Short-term deferred tax liabilities	516	165
Current liabilities of discontinued operations	0	124
Total current liabilities	9,212	8,643
Long-term debt and capitalized lease obligations	2,088	2,344
Pension and postretirement benefits	2,738	2,151
Other long-term liabilities	2,186	2,207
Long-term deferred tax liabilities	816	0
Non-current liabilities of discontinued operations	0	401
Total liabilities	17,040	15,746
Preferred stock, 20 shares authorized; none outstanding	-	-
Common stock $0.01 par value, 500 shares authorized;		
106 and 109 shares outstanding, respectively	1	1
Treasury stock, at cost	(5,981)	(5,826)
Capital in excess of par value	10,005	10,185
Retained earnings	1,865	4,930
Other comprehensive loss	(1,609)	(779)
Total Sears Holdings Corporation equity	4,281	8,511
Noncontrolling interest	60	103
Total equity	4,341	8,614
Total liabilities and equity	22,381	24,360

Sears Holdings Company
Consolidation Statements of Operations

	Jan 28, 2012	Jan 29, 2011	Jan 30, 2010
Merchandise sales and services	41,567	42,664	43,360
Costs and Expenses:			
Costs of sales, buying and occupancy	30,966	31,000	31,374
Selling and administrative	10,664	10,425	10,499
Depreciation and administrative	853	869	894
Impairment charges	649	0	0
Gain on sale of assets	(64)	(67)	(74)
Total costs and expenses	43,068	42,227	42,693
Operating income (loss)	(1,501)	437	667
Interest expense	(289)	(293)	(248)
Interest and investment income	41	36	33
Other loss, net	(2)	(14)	(61)
Income (loss) from continuing operations			
before income taxes	(1,751)	166	391
Income tax expense	(1,369)	(27)	(111)
Income (loss) from continuing operations	(3,120)	139	280
Income (loss) from discontinued operations	(27)	11	17
Net Income (Loss)	(3,147)	150	297
Basic and diluted EPS:	($29.40)	$1.19	$1.99

Example 11-5 presents the balance sheets for PepsiCo, Inc. using primarily historical costs. Total stockholders' equity reported on the balance sheet is not equal to the fair market value of PepsiCo, Inc because of the following (all amounts are in millions):

1) Inventories are stated at historical cost. The amount of $3,372 is not the net cash that is expected to be received from selling the products to customers.

2) Receivables is an estimated amount of what is expected to be collected from customers.

3) Property, plant, and equipment, net is reported at cost less accumulated depreciation. The amount does not represent the amount the assets are expected to generate in future cash flow.

4) Goodwill is reported at the amount paid to purchase another company over and above the fair market value of the net assets purchased. The amount does not represent the current future cash flows expected to be generated from the assets.

5) Liabilities are reported at the unpaid principle amount on the balance sheet date.

Example 11-5 continued:

6) Common stock and capital represents the amount that was initially contributed to the company for ownership. The amount does not represent the fair value of the stock.

7) The ability to generate ongoing profits from the business is not reported on the balance sheet.

PepsiCo, Inc. BALANCE SHEETS

(In millions)

June 30,		2011		2010
Assets				
Current assets:				
Cash and cash equivalents	$	**5,943**	$	3,943
Short-term investments		**426**		192
Inventories		**3,372**		2,618
Receivables		**7,828**		5,818
Total current assets		**17,569**		12,571
		19,058		
Property, plant and equipment, net				12,671
Investments		**1,368**		4,484
Goodwill		**14,661**		6,534
Intangible assets, net		**13,808**		2,623
Other long-term assets		**1,689**		965
Total assets	$	**68,153**	$	39,848
Liabilities and stockholders' equity				
Accounts payable and other	$	**10,923**	$	8,127
Short-term obligations		**4,898**		464
XXXXXXXXXXXXXXX		**71**		165
Total current liabilities		**15,892**		8,756
Long-term debt		**19,999**		7,400
XXXXXXXXXXXXX		**10,776**		6,250
Total liabilities		**46,677**		22,406
Commitments and contingencies				
Stockholders' equity:				
Stock and paid-in capital		**4,449**		176
Retained Earnings		**37,090**		33,805
Treasury Stock		**(16,745)**		(13,383)
Accumulated other comprehensive income		**(3,630)**		(3,794)
XXXXXXXXXX		**312**		638
Total Stockholders' equity		**21,476**		17,442
Total liabilities and stockholders' equity		**68,153**		39,848

Example 11-5 continued:

Consolidated Statement of Income
PepsiCo, Inc. and Subsidiaries

Fiscal years ended December 31
(in millions except per share amounts)

	2011	2010	2009
Net Revenue	**$ 66,504**	$ 57,838	$ 43,232
Cost of sales	**31,593**	26,575	20,099
Selling, general and administrative expenses	**25,145**	22,814	15,026
Amortization of intangible assets	**133**	117	63
Operating Profit	**9,633**	8,332	8,044
Bottling equity income	—	735	365
Interest expense	**(856)**	(903)	(397)
Interest income and other	**57**	68	67
Income before income taxes	**8,834**	8,232	8,079
Provision for income taxes	**2,372**	1,894	2,100
Net income	**6,462**	6,338	5,979
Less: Net income of noncontrolling interests	**19**	18	33
Net Income Attributable to PepsiCo	**$ 6,443**	$ 6,320	$ 5,946
Net Income Attributable to PepsiCo per Common Share			
Basic	**$ 4.08**	$ 3.97	$ 3.81
Diluted	**$ 4.03**	$ 3.91	$ 3.77
Weighted-average common shares outstanding			
Basic	**1,576**	1,590	1,558
Diluted	**1,597**	1,614	1,577

PepsiCo. Inc had a fair market value for the entire company on December 31, 2011 of the following:

	Number of shares of common stock outstanding	1,570	million
x	Fair market value per common share	$66.35	
=	Total fair market value of the company	$104.2	billion
-	Book value (equity) on the balance sheet	$21.476	billion
=	Difference in book value and fair market value	$82.724	billion

Investors expect PepsiCo. Inc. to earn approximately $5.00 per share for 2012; a total of $7.9 billion in earnings for the company.

$$\frac{\text{Difference in book value and fair market value}}{\text{Expected earnings for PepsiCo., Inc.}} \quad \frac{\$82.727 \text{ billion}}{\$ \ 7.9 \text{ billion}} = 10.5 \text{ x earnings}$$

Investors are willing to pay for more than 10 years of future earnings at the current fair market value. Investors are willing to pay over $80 billion now for the expectation that PepsiCo. Inc. will earn more than $80 billion in future years.

Example 11-6 presents the balance sheet and income statement for Facebook, Inc. as presented in the Form S-1 filed with the Securities Exchange Commission in April 2012, before offering to sell shares of the company to the general public. Potential investors used the financial statements and other information in the Form S-1 to estimate the fair market value of one share of common stock.

The balance sheet shows total stockholders' equity (net book value) for the entire company of $5.228 billion. Investors purchased shares on the first day the stock was publicly traded for approximately $40 per share, giving the total company a fair market value of approximately $80 billion. Immediately after the initial public offering there were approximately two billion shares of common stock.

At a total fair market value of $80 billion, investors are willing to pay for the next 120 years of earnings. Investors are willing to pay for 60 years of earnings if earnings double and 30 years of earnings if earnings quadruple. Investors are expecting earnings to grow significantly if they are willing to pay a total of $80 billion for the entire company.

$$\frac{\text{Total estimated fair market value of the company}}{\text{Total earnings during fiscal year 2011 to common stockholders}} = \frac{\$80 \text{ billion}}{\$668 \text{ million}} = 120 \text{ years}$$

The balance sheet for Facebook, Inc. reports just over $6 billion in total assets, including slightly more than $1.7 billion book value for long-term assets. Investors are giving very little weight to the book value of assets when estimating the total fair market value of Facebook, Inc. The company's total fair market value of $80 billion is based on the expected future earnings of the entire company.

FACEBOOK, INC.
CONSOLIDATED BALANCE SHEETS
(In millions, except for number of shares and par value)

	December 31, 2010	December 31, 2011	Pro Forma December 31, 2011 (unaudited)
Assets			
Cash and cash equivalents	$1,785	$1,512	$ 1,512
Marketable securities	—	2,396	2,396
Accounts receivable, net of allowances for doubtful accounts of $11 and $17 as of December 31, 2010 and 2011, respectively	373	547	547
Prepaid expenses and other current assets	88	149	478
Total current assets	2,246	4,604	4,933
Property and equipment, net	574	1,475	1,475
Goodwill and intangible assets, net	96	162	162
Other assets	74	90	90
Total assets	$2,990	$6,331	$ 6,660
Liabilities and stockholders' equity			
Accounts payable	$ 29	$ 63	$ 63
Platform partners payable	75	171	171
Accrued expenses and other current liabilities	137	296	296
Deferred revenue and deposits	42	90	90
Current portion of capital lease obligations	106	279	279
Total current liabilities	389	899	899
Capital lease obligations, less current portion	117	398	398
Long-term debt	250	—	—
Other liabilities	72	135	135
Total liabilities	828	1,432	1,432
Commitments and contingencies			
Stockholders' equity:			
Convertible preferred stock, $0.000006 par value, issuable in series: 569 million shares authorized, 541 million and 543 million shares issued and outstanding at December 31, 2010 and 2011, respectively (aggregate liquidation preference of $615 million as of December 31, 2011); no shares authorized, issued and outstanding, pro forma	615	615	—
Common stock, $0.000006 par value: 4,141 million Class A shares authorized, 60 million shares issued and outstanding at December 31, 2010, and 117 million shares issued and outstanding, including 1 million outstanding shares subject to repurchase at December 31, 2011 and pro forma; 4,141 million Class B shares authorized, 1,112 million, 1,213 million and 1,759 million shares issued and outstanding, including 5 million, 2 million and 2 million outstanding shares subject to repurchase, at December 31, 2010, 2011 and pro forma, respectively	—	—	—
Additional paid-in capital	947	2,684	4,267
Accumulated other comprehensive loss	(6)	(6)	(6)
Retained earnings	606	1,606	967
Total stockholders' equity	2,162	4,899	5,228
Total liabilities and stockholders' equity	$2,990	$6,331	$ 6,660

FACEBOOK, INC.
CONSOLIDATED STATEMENTS OF INCOME
(In millions, except per share amounts)

	Year Ended December 31,		
	2009	2010	2011
Revenue	$ 777	$1,974	$3,711
Costs and expenses:			
Cost of revenue	223	493	860
Marketing and sales	115	184	427
Research and development	87	144	388
General and administrative	90	121	280
Total costs and expenses	515	942	1,955
Income from operations	262	1,032	1,756
Other expense, net:			
Interest expense	(10)	(22)	(42)
Other income (expense), net	2	(2)	(19)
Income before provision for income taxes	254	1,008	1,695
Provision for income taxes	25	402	695
Net income	$ 229	$ 606	$1,000
Net income attributable to participating securities	107	234	332
Net income attributable to Class A and Class B common stockholders	$ 122	$ 372	$ 668
Earnings per share attributable to Class A and Class B common stockholders:			
Basic	$0.12	$ 0.34	$ 0.52
Diluted	$0.10	$ 0.28	$ 0.46

See Notes to Consolidated Financial Statements.

F-4

145

FACEBOOK, INC.
CONSOLIDATED STATEMENTS OF CASH FLOWS
(In millions)

| | Year Ended December 31, | | |
	2009	2010	2011
Cash flows from operating activities			
Net income	$ 229	$ 606	$ 1,000
Adjustments to reconcile net income to net cash			
Depreciation and amortization	78	139	323
Loss on write-off of equipment	1	3	4
Share-based compensation	27	20	217
Tax benefit from share-based award activity	50	115	433
Excess tax benefit from share-based award activity	(51)	(115)	(433)
Changes in assets and liabilities:			
Accounts receivable	(112)	(209)	(174)
Prepaid expenses and other current assets	(30)	(38)	(31)
Other assets	(59)	17	(32)
Accounts payable	(7)	12	6
Platform partners payable	—	75	96
Accrued expenses and other current liabilities	27	20	38
Deferred revenue and deposits	1	37	49
Other liabilities	1	16	53
Net cash provided by operating activities	155	698	1,549
Cash flows from investing activities			
Purchases of property and equipment	(33)	(293)	(606)
Purchases of marketable securities	—	—	(3,025)
Maturities of marketable securities	—	—	516
Sales of marketable securities	—	—	113
Investments in non-marketable equity securities	—	—	(3)
Acquisitions of business, net of cash acquired, and purchases of intangible and other assets	3	(22)	(24)
Change in restricted cash and deposits	(32)	(9)	6
Net cash used in investing activities	(62)	(324)	(3,023)
Cash flows from financing activities			
Net proceeds from issuance of convertible preferred stock	200	—	—
Net proceeds from issuance of common stock	—	500	998
Proceeds from exercise of stock options	9	6	28
Proceeds from (repayments of) long-term debt	—	250	(250)
Proceeds from sale and lease-back transactions	31	—	170
Principal payments on capital lease obligations	(48)	(90)	(181)
Excess tax benefit from share-based award activity	51	115	433
Net cash provided by financing activities	243	781	1,198
Effect of exchange rate changes on cash and cash equivalents	—	(3)	3
Net increase (decrease) in cash and cash equivalents	336	1,152	(273)
Cash and cash equivalents at beginning of period	297	633	1,785
Cash and cash equivalents at end of period	$ 633	$1,785	$ 1,512
Supplemental cash flow data			
Cash paid during the period for:			
Interest	$ 9	$ 23	$ 28
Income taxes	$ 42	$ 261	$ 197
Non-cash investing and financing activities:			
Property and equipment additions included in accounts payable and accrued expenses and other liabilities	$ 5	$ 47	$ 135
Property and equipment acquired under capital leases	$ 56	$ 217	$ 473
Fair value of shares issued related to acquisitions of business and other assets	$ 20	$ 60	$ 58

Appendix A

A-1 Recording Business Transactions

It is the responsibility of the financial accountant to prepare and provide financial information to people making financial decisions; management, investors, and creditors. Financial information is prepared by recording and summarizing all the individual transactions of the company. The detail recording of transactions is done for internal purposes only and is not provided to anyone outside the accounting department.

All transactions are an exchange of one thing for another thing. An **account** is the name of the item that changes when a transaction occurs. Account names are used to record each transaction and summarize amounts. Most companies use a standard chart of accounts that lists the account names commonly used to record and summarize transactions. Account names were discussed in chapters 2 through 6.

Every transaction changes the accounting equation. The accounting equation must always stay in balance. Assets are either owned or the company owes for them.

The Accounting Equation

Assets	=	**Liabilities**	+	**Stockholders' Equity**
Have	=	Owe	+	Own Includes retained earnings (Revenues, expenses, gains and losses = net Earnings)

The earnings of the company belong to the owners. Earnings become part of retained earnings. Revenues, expenses, gains and losses are sub accounts of retained earnings, which is included in stockholders' equity.

Four common transactions that **change the balance sheet** are as follows:

1) Receive cash from investors in exchange for ownership.
2) Trade an asset for another asset (includes paying cash for another asset.)
3) Receive an asset and pay for the asset in the future (increase a liability.)
4) Pay cash to reduce amounts owed (decrease a liability.)

The following steps should be taken to record the exchange associated with each transaction that changes the balance sheet:

1) Determine what was <u>received</u> and the account name that describes it.

2) Determine what was <u>given</u> in exchange and the account name that describes it.

Common balance sheet account names include the following:

Assets the company has:

Cash
Accounts receivable
Inventory
Prepaid expense (insurance, rent)
Short-term investments
Short-term notes receivable
Supplies
Long-term investments
Long-term notes receivable
Land
Buildings
Equipment
Autos (Vehicles)
Computer equipment
Goodwill
Trademarks
Copyrights
Patents

Liabilities the company owes:

Accounts payable
Accrued expenses
Accrued liabilities
Short-term notes payable
Rent payable
Salaries payable (Wages payable)
Interest payable
Unearned revenues
Warranty payable
Dividends payable
Taxes payable
Long-term debt
Long-term notes payable
Current maturities of notes payable
    or long-term debt

Stockholders' Equity: (Represents ownership)

Stock
Capital or Paid in Capital
Retained Earnings
Treasury Stock

A spreadsheet can be used to record transactions. Each transaction is recorded on a separate line (row.) Make sure the accounting equation stays in balance (assets = liabilities + stockholders' equity) on each row. The common account names that describe what is received or given in exchange is written at the top of the column. The amount is put in the column name that is affected. A positive number indicates an increase and a negative number indicates a decrease for balance sheet items. The order the account names are placed on the spreadsheet does not matter. It is helpful to group all assets and all liabilities and all stockholders' equity together.

Example A1-1 illustrates the use of a spreadsheet to record balance sheet transactions. Three transactions that occurred when the company began business are recorded on a spreadsheet as follows:

1) The company issued stock to investors for $100,000.
2) The company purchased inventory on account in the amount of $12,000.
3) The company purchased furniture for cash in the amount of $10,000.

	Cash	Inventory	Furniture	=	Accounts Payable	+	Common Stock
1)	$100,000			=			$100,000
2)		$12,000		=	$12,000		
3)	($10,000)		$10,000	=			
Total	$90,000	$12,000	$10,000	=	$12,000		$100,000

$112,000 Total Assets = $12,000 Liabilities + $100,000 Stockholders' Equity

The accounting equation must remain in balance as each transaction is recorded.

Total each account column after all transactions that occurred during the period are recorded. The total amount in each account is reported on the balance sheet at the end of the period.

Assets:		Liabilities:	
Cash	$ 90,000	Accounts Payable	$ 12,000
Inventory	$ 12,000		
Total Current Assets	$102,000		
		Stockholders' Equity:	
Property and Equipment:		Common Stock	$100,000
Furniture	$ 10,000		
		Total Liabilities and	
Total Assets	$112,000	Stockholders' Equity	$112,000

Example 3-1, on page 34-38 provides an additional example of recording balance sheet transactions on a spreadsheet.

There are three general transactions that occur that change the income statement. A transaction that changes the income statement will <u>also</u> change the balance sheet.

1st record the revenue or expense

2nd record the balance sheet account that <u>also</u> changes.

1) The Company <u>provides</u> goods or services to customers (always in exchange for an asset)

<u>Income Statement</u>   <u>Balance Sheet</u>

Revenue   Unearned revenue decreases if the cash was
                                   received in a prior period.

                    or   Cash increases if cash is received in the
                                   same period.

                    or   A receivable increases if cash will
                                   be received in a future period.

2) The company <u>receives</u> a service (in exchange for an asset to pay for it)

<u>Income Statement</u>   <u>Balance Sheet</u>

Expense   Prepaid expense is reduced if cash was
                                   paid in a prior period.

                    or   Cash decreases if cash is paid in the same period.

                    or   Accounts payable, xxx payable or accrued liability
                                   increases if cash will be paid in a future period.

3) The company uses an asset in order to provide goods or services to customers

<u>Income Statement</u>   <u>Balance Sheet</u>

Expense   The asset used decreases:
                              Prepaid expense
                              Supplies
                              Inventory
                              Property and equipment (accumulated depreciation)
                              Intangible assets (accumulated amortization)

150

Use the following as a general guide to determine the account name to use when recording transactions that change both the balance sheet and the income statement.

Goods or services are <u>provided to a customer.</u>

    1) Goods provided are called **sales.**

    2) Services provided is called **revenue or fees.**

    3) Providing the use of an asset is called a revenue name that represents what is provided. Examples of this are rent revenue (providing excess space used by others) and interest revenue (provide funds to be used by others.)

A service is <u>provided to the company</u>.

Name of the expense	Service that was provided
Utilities expense	Electricity, water, and other utilities
Salaries or wages expense	Employees worked
Insurance expense	Coverage for liability, property damage, etc.
Rent expense	Use of an asset owned by others
Advertising expense	Promoting the business to potential customers
Interest expense	The use of another's money

An <u>asset is used (up)</u> to provide goods or services to customers.

    1) Using up **<u>inventory</u>** is called **<u>cost of goods sold.</u>**

    2) Using up **<u>prepaid expenses</u>** is called the **<u>name of the prepaid</u>** that is no longer. Examples are insurance expense, rent expense and advertising expense.

    3) Using up **<u>supplies</u>** is called **<u>supplies expense.</u>**

    4) Using owned **<u>property and equipment</u>** is called **<u>depreciation expense.</u>**

    5) Using owned **<u>intangible assets</u>** is called **<u>amortization expense.</u>**

Remember the following:

    1) Revenue also increases an asset **or** decreases unearned revenue.

    2) An expense also decreases an asset **or** increases a liability.

    3) A revenue and an expense do not both change in the same exchange.

Revenue, expense, gain, loss, and dividend accounts must also be included on the spreadsheet or the accounting equation will not remain in balance. These accounts are listed under stockholders' equity because they will be reported as part of retained earnings.

Total stockholders' equity includes all of the following accounts:

	Stock	R. E.	Revenues	(Expense)	Gains	(Losses)	(Dividends)
Beg.	$1,000	$29,000					

Each different type of revenue and gain account has its own column.
    Revenues are recorded with a **positive** number because revenue increases earnings.

Each different type of expense and loss account has its own column.
    Expenses are recorded with a **negative** number because expenses decrease earnings.

Dividends reduce retained earnings and are recorded with a **negative** number.
    Dividends is a return of capital to the owners and is not an expense.

All revenue, expense, gain, loss, and dividend accounts are reported as part of retained earnings at the end of the period. **Retained earnings** is the net of cumulative earnings and cumulative dividends paid to owners. Cumulative means including everything from the first day the company began business.

The amount of retained earnings reported on the balance sheet includes the current period profits and losses and the current period dividends to owners.

	Beginning Retained Earnings (prior period ending balance)
+	Net earnings for the current period
-	Dividends to owners during the current period
=	Retained Earnings reported on the balance sheet (current period0

Example A1-2 illustrates the use of a spreadsheet to record income statement and balance sheet transactions. This is not the first year of business and the company has beginning balances for items reported on the balance sheet (assets, liabilities, and retained earnings.) Income statement accounts begin with zero because amounts are for the current period only. Three transactions occurred during the current period as follows:

1) The company sold inventory that cost $10,000 for $14,000, on account to customers.
2) Employees earned $1,100 and the company paid the employees.
3) The company received a utility bill for $220 for the current period service.

The three transactions are recorded on the spreadsheet as follows:

| | Assets | | | = | Liabilities | + Stockholders' Equity | |
	Cash	Accounts Receivable	Inventory	=	Accounts Payable	Common Stock	Retained Earnings
Beg.	$10,000	$5,000	$22,000		$8,000	$1,000	$28,000
1)		14,000	(10,000)	=			
2)	(1,100)			=			
3)				=	220		
Total	$ 8,900	$19,000	$12,000	=	$8,220	$1,000	$28,000

+ Stockholders' Equity: Revenues less Expenses = Profits Included in Retained Earnings

	Sales	(Cost of Goods Sold)	(Salaries Expense)	(Utilities Expense)
Beg.				
1)	14,000	(10,000)		
2)			(1,100)	
3)				(220)
	$14,000	($10,000)	($1,100)	($220)

153

Example A1-2 continued:

The balance sheet reports the following:

Assets:		Liabilities:	
Cash	$ 8,900	Accounts Payable	$ 8,220
Accounts Receivable	19,000		
Inventory	12,000		
Total Current Assets	$ 39,900		
		Stockholders' Equity:	
		Common Stock	$ 1,000
		Retained Earnings	30,680
		Total Stockholders' Equity	$31,680
		Total Liabilities and	
Total Assets	$ 39,900	Stockholders' Equity	$39,900

The income statement reports the following:

Sales	$14,000	
Cost of Goods Sold	(10,000)	
Gross Profit	4,000	
Salaries Expense	(1,100)	
Utilities Expense	(220)	
Net Income	2,680	included in retained earnings

The retained earnings column on the statement of stockholders' equity will report the following:

Beginning Retained Earnings	$28,000	
+ Net Income	2,680	from the income statement
- Dividends	0	
= Ending Retained Earnings	$30,680	reported on the balance sheet above

Example 6-5 on pages 76 to 81 provides an additional example of recording income statement transactions that also change the balance sheet.

154

A-2 Record Journal Entries and Balance Accounts

The spreadsheet is a useful tool for recording and summarizing transactions when there are only a few transactions. Many companies today have thousands of transactions and use hundreds of different account names. A spreadsheet used to record transactions becomes too large to be printed in a way that is easy to read.

Accountants created a method of recording transactions that can be written on one page at a time. This method, called **double entry bookkeeping**, was documented by Venetian merchants in Italy in 1494. Double entry bookkeeping is the method used today to record transactions either by hand or using computer systems and software. **Journal entries** are used to record the change to each account for every transaction. Amounts recorded in journal entries are summarized in "T" accounts and totaled to obtain the final amounts reported on financial statements.

Examples of journal entries that record transactions are as follows:

1) Cash $100,000
      Common Stock $100,000

Ownership is issued in exchange for cash.

2) Computers $ 5,000
    Furniture $10,000
      Cash $15,000

Computers and Furniture are purchased for cash.

3) Equipment $30,000
      Cash $18,000
      Notes Payable $12,000

Equipment is purchased partially for cash with an agreement to pay the difference in the future.

The account name written on top is called a **debit**. The account name written on bottom, indented to the right, is called a **credit.** Total debit amounts (top) must equal total credit amounts (bottom.) Each journal entry must have at least one debit and at least one credit and can have more than one debit or credit. Total debits must equal total credits.

The words **debit** and **credit** have no specific meaning except to describe how a journal entry is written.

All amounts in journal entries are positive numbers.

Each account name has a separate "T" account. It is called a "T" account because a T is drawn first and amounts are entered on the left or right.

Debit amounts are written on the left. Credit amounts are written on the right.

Account Name	
Debit	Credit
Amounts	Amounts

Whether an amount is a debit or a credit, depends on what type of account is changing and if it is increasing or decreasing.

Assets and expenses increase with a debit, decrease with a credit, and should always have a total net amount on the debit side.

Asset or Expense	
Debit	Credit
Amounts	Amounts
↑	↓
Net	

ADE

Debit	Credit
+	−

Stockholders' equity, liabilities and revenues increase with a credit, decrease with a debit, and should always have a total net amount on the credit side.

Stockholders' Equity, Liability or Revenue	
Debit	Credit
Amounts	Amounts
↓	↑
	Net

LOCR

debit	credit
−	+

156

Journal entries are recorded using the following steps:

1) Determine the account names that change because of the transaction.

2) Determine the category of each account name that is changing (asset, liability, stockholders' equity, revenue, expense.)

3) Determine if the change to each account name is an increase or a decrease.

4) Use the T account guide (increases and decreases) to determine if the change is a debit or credit for each account.

5) Write all debit account names on the top.
   Write all credit account names on the bottom, indented to the right.
   See the previous example for the format of a journal entry.

All transactions are an exchange. In most cases, the debit is the benefit the company receives and the credit is the item the company gives up to get the benefit.

> Account name benefit or service **received** $$$
>   Account name **given up** to get it $$$

Follow these steps to summarize final numbers for the financial statements after recording journal entries:

1) Draw a "T" and write the account name on the top of the T.
   Do this for <u>each</u> account name used.

2) Put all amounts in the journal entries in the "T" account of the name of the account used.

   Write all debit amounts (top) on the left side of the appropriate T account.

   Write all credit amounts (bottom) on the right side of the appropriate T account.

3) Total the debits amounts on the left side and the credits amounts on the right side. Write the subtotal amount for each side.

4) Subtract the smallest subtotal amount from the largest subtotal amount, and **write the difference on the largest subtotal's side.** Subtracting the smallest amount from the largest amount is the same thing as netting the increases and the decreases.

Examples A2-1 and A2-2-2 illustrate how to record journal entries and balance T accounts.

Example A2-1: BGJ, Inc. had three transactions during the first month of operations that change the balance sheet only. The transactions are recorded in journal entries.

1) The company received $20,000 cash from owners in exchange for ownership in the company.

	Cash	**Common stock**
a) Which account names change?		
b) What type of account is changing?	Asset	Stockholders' equity
c) Is the change to each account an increase or a decrease?	Increase	Increase
d) Is the change to each account a debit or credit?	Debit	Credit

```
Cash                        20,000
        Common Stock                 20,000
```

2) The company signed a note at the bank and received cash of $8,000. The total is to be repaid in 18 months.

	Cash	**Long-term notes payable**
a) Which account names change?		
b) What type of account is changing?	Asset	Liability
c) Is the change to each account an increase or a decrease?	Increase	Increase
d) Is the change to each account a debit or credit?	Debit	Credit

```
Cash                           8,000
        Long-term notes payable        8,000
```

3) The company paid $2,000 cash for office furniture.

	Office furniture	**Cash**
a) Which account names change?		
b) What type of account is changing?	Asset	Asset
c) Is the change to each account an increase or a decrease?	Increase	Decrease
d) Is the change to each account a debit or credit?	Debit	Credit

```
Office Furniture               2,000
        Cash                           2,000
```

158

Example A2-1 continued

The amounts recorded in each journal entry are written in the T account with the account name written at the top. Debit amounts are on the left side and credit amounts are on the right side.

Subtotal each side and subtract the smallest amount from the largest amount. The final total will be on the side that increases. The T accounts are formatted as follows:

	Cash	
20,000		
8,000	2,000	
28,000	2,000	
26,000		

Office Furniture			Common Stock			Long-term Notes Payable	
2,000				20,000			8,000
2,000				20,000			8,000

Each account name used and the final balance are reported on the balance sheet as follows:

Assets:		Liabilities:	
Cash	$26,000	Long-term Notes Payable	$ 8,000
Office Furniture	$ 2,000		
		Stockholders' Equity:	
		Common Stock	$ 20,000
		Total Liabilities and	
Total Assets	$28,000	Stockholders' Equity	$28,000

Example A2-2: BGJ, Inc. had the following transactions during January, the first month of operations, that change the balance sheet and the income statement. The transactions are recorded in journal entries.

1) The company purchased inventory for $18,000, on account.

	Inventory	**Accounts Payable**
a) Which account names change?		
b) What type of account is changing?	Asset	Liability
c) Is the change to each account an increase or a decrease?	Increase	Increase
d) Is the change to each account a debit or credit?	Debit	Credit

    Inventory $18,000
         Accounts Payable $18,000

2) The company sold inventory that cost $10,000 to customers for $17,500, on account.

	Inventory	**Cost of Goods Sold**
a) Which account names change?		
b) What type of account is changing?	Asset	Expense
c) Is the change to each account an increase or a decrease?	Decrease	Increase
d) Is the change to each account a debit or credit?	Credit	Debit

	Accounts Receivable	**Sales**
a) Which account names change?		
b) What type of account is changing?	Asset	Revenue
c) Is the change to each account an increase or a decrease?	Increase	Increase
d) Is the change to each account a debit or credit?	Debit	Credit

    Cost of Goods Sold $10,000
         Inventory $10,000
    Accounts Receivable $17,500
         Sales $17,500

3) Employees worked this period and were paid $1,100.

	Salary Expense	**Cash**
a) Which account names change?		
b) What type of account is changing?	Expense	Asset
c) Is the change to each account an increase or a decrease?	Increase	Decrease
d) Is the change to each account a debit or credit?	Debit	Credit

    Salary Expense $1,100
         Cash $1,100

160

Example A2-2 continued

4) The company received a utility bill for $200 for services provided during January.

	Utilities Expense	Accounts Payable
a) Which account names change?		
b) What type of account is changing?	Expense	Liability
c) Is the change to each account an increase or a decrease?	Increase	Increase
d) Is the change to each account a debit or credit?	Debit	Credit

Utilities Expense $200
     Accounts Payable $200

5) The company paid for insurance for three months (beginning with January), at a total cost of $3,000.

	Cash	Prepaid Insurance	Insurance Expense
a) Which account names change?			
b) What type of account is changing?	Asset	Asset	Expense
c) Is the change to each account an increase or a decrease?	Decrease	Increase	Increase
d) Is the change to each account a debit or credit?	Credit	Debit	Debit

Prepaid Insurance $2,000 (February and March)
Insurance Expense $1,000 (January)
     Cash $3,000

6) The company collected $8,000 from customers who previously owed on account.

	Cash	Accounts Receivable
a) Which account names change?		
b) What type of account is changing?	Asset	Asset
c) Is the change to each account an increase or a decrease?	Increase	Decrease
d) Is the change to each account a debit or credit?	Debit	Credit

Cash $8,000
     Accounts Receivable $8,000

7) The company paid $500 for advertising services provided during the current month.

	Cash	Advertising Expense
a) Which account names change?		
b) What type of account is changing?	Asset	Expense
c) Is the change to each account an increase or a decrease?	Decrease	Increase
d) Is the change to each account a debit or credit?	Credit	Debit

Advertising Expense $500
     Cash $500

Example A2-2 continued

8) The company invested $5,000 cash in short-term investments.

		Cash	S/T Investments
a)	Which account names change?	**Cash**	**S/T Investments**
b)	What type of account is changing?	Asset	Asset
c)	Is the change to each account an increase or a decrease?	Decrease	Increase
d)	Is the change to each account a debit or credit?	Credit	Debit

S/T Investments	$5,000	
Cash		$5,000

9) Income tax expense for the month is $1,200. The expense has not been paid.

		Income Tax Expense	Income Tax Payable
a)	Which account names change?	**Income Tax Expense**	**Income Tax Payable**
b)	What type of account is changing?	Expense	Liability
c)	Is the change to each account an increase or a decrease?	Increase	Increase
d)	Is the change to each account a debit or credit?	Debit	Credit

Income Tax Expense	$1,200	
Income Tax Payable		$1,200

All journal entries made in examples A2-1 and A2-2 are put into T accounts and balanced.

	Cash					Office Furniture				Common Stock	
13-1	20,000				13-1	2,000				20,000	13-1
13-1	8,000	2,000	13-1								
		1,100	(3)								
		3,000	(5)			2,000				20,000	
(6)	8,000										
		500	(7)								
		5,000	(8)								
	36,000	11,600									
	24,400										

162

Example A2-2 continued

Inventory

(1)	18,000	10,000	(2)
	8,000		

Accounts Payable

		18,000	(1)
		200	(4)
		18,200	

Long-term Notes Payable

		8,000	13-1
		8,000	

Cost of Goods Sold

(2)	10,000	
	10,000	

Accounts Receivable

(2)	17,500	8,000	(6)
	9,500		

Sales

		17,500	(2)
		17,500	

Utility Expense

(4)	200	
	200	

Income Tax Expense

(9)	1,200	
	1,200	

Salary Expense

(3)	1,100	
	1,100	

Advertising Expense

(7)	500	
	500	

Prepaid Insurance

(5)	2,000	
	2,000	

Insurance Expense

(5)	1,000	
	1,000	

163

Example A2-2 continued

Short-term Investments		Income Tax Payable	
(8) 5,000			1,200 (9)
5,000			1,200

Financial statements are prepared using all accounts and amounts summarized in T accounts.

The income statement will report the following:

	Sales	17,500
-	Cost of Goods Sold	(10,000)
=	Gross Profit	7,500
-	Operating Expenses	
	Utilities	(200)
	Salaries	(1,100)
	Advertising	(500)
	Insurance	(1,000)
=	Income Before Taxes	4,700
	Income Tax Expense	(1,200)
=	Net Income	3,500 included in retained earnings

The balance sheet will report the following:

Assets:		Liabilities:	
Cash	24,400	Accounts Payable	18,200
Accounts Receivable	9,500	Income Taxes Payable	1,200
Inventory	8,000	Total Current Liabilities	19,400
Prepaid Insurance	2,000		
Short-term Investments	5,000	Long-term Notes Payable	8,000
Total Current Assets	48,900	Total Liabilities	27,400
Office Furniture	2,000	Stockholders' Equity:	
		Common Stock	20,000
		Retained Earnings	3,500
		Total Stockholders' Equity	23,500
Total Assets	50,900	Total Liabilities and	
		Stockholders' Equity	50,900

164

Contra asset accounts are reported in the asset section and reduce other asset accounts. Contra asset accounts are recorded opposite of the way an asset account is recorded as follows:

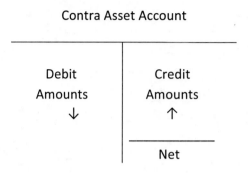

Contra Asset Account

Debit Amounts ↓	Credit Amounts ↑
	Net

The cost of using a long-term asset is recorded as follows:

Depreciation Expense $$$
      Accumulated Depreciation $$$

Accumulated depreciation is a contra asset that increases with a credit.

The amount of accounts receivable that is not expected to be collected is recorded as follows:

Bad Debt Expense $$$
      Allowance for Uncollectible Accounts $$$

Allowance for uncollectible accounts is a contra asset that increases with a credit.

Journal entries and T accounts are used by accountants to record and summarize transactions. Final balances are reported on the financial statements. Prior to the use of computers, all entries were hand written and balanced. Today, journal entries are entered into the computer system and the software automatically creates the T account and totals each account.

A computer report, called a detail general ledger, provides the detail of all the increases and decreases to each account and the final balance. A summary general ledger, similar to the adjusted trial balance discussed in Appendix A-4, reports the final balance for all accounts.

The detail of the recorded transactions is maintained by accountants and is not provided to anyone outside the accounting department. Summarized accounts and amounts are reported in the format of financial statements. Financial statements and footnotes are provided to investors and creditors.

165

A-3 Adjustments to Accounts

The accounting department has standard procedures and processes in place to identify and record transactions that occur repeatedly. Providing goods to customers occurs daily. Common standard procedures and the accounting entries that are made as the process occurs, follows:

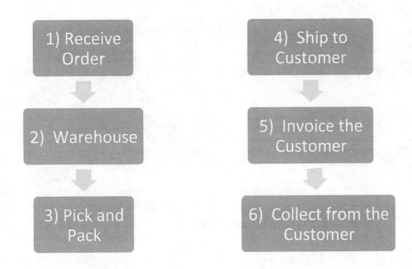

1) An order is received and entered into the computer system; the customer service representative enters the order or the customer directly enters the order online.

2) The warehouse receives the order and prints a "pick ticket" that lists the customer information and the items that must be shipped to the customer.

3) Warehouse personnel pick the items off the shelf and pack them in a box ready for shipping.

4) The package is shipped to the customer. Warehouse personnel enter a "ship confirm" into the computer system. The computer system has record of the price to the customer and the cost of inventory sold and automatically records the sale as follows:

Accounts Receivable	$$$		Cost of Goods Sold	$$$
Sales		$$$	Inventory	$$$

5) The customer is invoiced when the package is shipped. The customer name and amount is automatically added to the list of amounts owed by customers. This list agrees to the total amount of the accounts receivable account.

6) The customer pays the company in approximately 30 days. The accountant enters the receipt of the check as payment from the customer and the following journal entry is made:

Cash	$$$	
Accounts Receivable		$$$

The company receives goods and services daily. The process of paying for goods and services received and the accounting entries that are made as the process occurs follows:

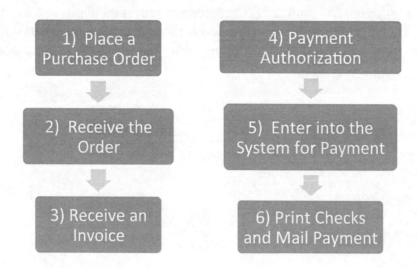

1) The company identifies goods or services that are required and the responsible functional manager places an order with a preapproved supplier.

2) The company receives the goods or services.

3) An invoice is received by the accounting department.

4) The accounting department sends the invoice to the responsible functional manager who verifies that the goods or services were received and authorizes the invoice for payment. The accounting department employee that processes payment is the accounts payable clerk.

5) The accounts payable clerk enters the invoice into the computer system for payment. The name of the supplier, the invoice number, the due date, the amount and the account name that will be reported (an asset name or an expense name*) is entered into the computer system. The computer system automatically enters the following journal entry:

Account Name *	$$$	
Accounts Payable		$$$

Entering invoices and selecting the account name is a critical step in the accounting process. All assets and services (expenses) purchased by the company are recorded in the accounting records with this step.

6) Checks are printed and mailed to the suppliers. The computer system automatically enters the following journal entry when checks are printed:

Accounts Payable	$$$	
Cash		$$$

168

Transactions recorded at the time the exchange takes place and an entry is made into the computer system is referred to as an "original entry" in this book. Large public companies do thousands of these transactions daily.

Why does a company need educated accountants if the accounting system does it all? The system records transactions related to goods and services provided to customers, cash receipts, and cash payments. **Transactions with no physical exchange are not automatically recorded by the computer system.** These transactions typically require judgments or estimates. The following transactions must be recorded by an accountant:

1) Assets used up and no longer available (prepaid expenses and supplies.)

2) The cost of using assets still available to use (long-term assets.)

3) Providing to customers that paid in a previous period (unearned revenue.)

4) Revenue earned as time passes and cash has not been received.
    (service revenue, interest revenue, dividend revenue, and rent revenue.)

5) Services received and the invoice has not yet been received.

6) Other expenses and losses that have not yet occurred and must be estimated.

Adjusting journal entries are made to record transactions the computer system does not automatically record during the period. Adjusting journal entries are made at the end of the period (month, quarter, year) before preparing financial statements.

Common transactions that require adjusting entries and the accounts name used are as follows:

1) Assets were used (up) during the period:

Supplies expense	and	Supplies
Cost of Goods Sold	and	Inventory
Depreciation expense	and	Accumulated Depreciation
Amortization expense	and	Accumulated Amortization

2) An expense was not recorded because an invoice was not received and the amount was not paid:

Salaries expense	and	Salaries payable
Interest expense	and	Interest payable
Tax expense	and	Tax payable
_____ expense	and	Accrued Liabilities

Common transactions that require adjusting entries and the accounts names (continued):

3) Revenues were not recorded because no documentation was received by the accounting department or an entry was not made in the system:

Sales (goods)	and	Accounts receivable
Service revenue	and	Accounts receivable
Revenue	and	Unearned revenue
		(if paid in a previous period)

4) A revenue or expense occurs as time passes:

Interest expense	and	Interest payable
Insurance expense	and	Prepaid insurance
Rent expense	and	Prepaid rent
Interest revenue	and	Interest receivable
Rent revenue	and	Rent receivable

Example A3-1 provides several examples of adjusting journal entries. The adjusting entries are made on **December 31st before preparing the annual financial statements.** Notice how the amount of the adjustment is determined.

1. The office supplies account had a balance of $1,450 on December 31st. The company counted office supplies at the end of the year and determined there were $920 of office supplies on hand.

	Office Supplies	Supplies Expense
a) Which account names change?		
b) What type of account is changing?	Asset	Expense
c) Is the change to each account an increase or a decrease?	Decrease	Increase
d) Is the change to each account a debit or credit?	Credit	Debit

What should the balance be on December 31st?

Office supplies is an asset. The balance should be the amount owned; $920.

Current balance	1,450
Balance should be	920
Adjustment needed	530 reduce office supplies

Using up an asset is an expense that must be recorded.

Make the adjusting entry to record the expense of using the asset.

Office supplies expense	$530	
Office supplies		$530

2. The company signed a six month lease to rent office space on September 1st. The company paid for the entire six months at a cost of $12,000 on September 1st and recorded the entire payment to prepaid rent.

	Prepaid Rent	**Rent Expense**
a) Which account names change?		
b) What type of account is changing?	Asset	Expense
c) Is the change to each account an increase or a decrease?	Decrease	Increase
d) Is the change to each account a debit or credit?	Credit	Debit

What should the balance be on December 31st?

Paid $12,000 for six months = $2,000 per month.

Two months are left and four months have been used up on December 31st.

Cost per month	$ 2,000
x Number of months passed	4
= Adjustment to be made	$ 8,000 used up = expense

Four months of prepaid rent have been used up and must be decreased and recorded as rent expense.

Make the adjusting entry to record the expense of using the space for time passed:

Rent Expense	$8,000	
Prepaid Rent		$8,000

3. On January 1st of <u>last year</u>, the company purchased a tractor for $100,000. The tractor is expected to be used for seven years and was used during the current year.

	Depreciation Expense	**Accumulated Depreciation**
a) Which account names change?		
b) What type of account is changing?	Expense	Contra Asset
c) Is the change to each account an increase or a decrease?	Increase	Increase
d) Is the change to each account a debit or credit?	Debit	Credit

What should be recorded on December 31st of the current year?

Cost $100,000 / 7 year life = $14,286 each year

Make the adjusting entry to record the expense of using the long-term asset.

Depreciation Expense	$14,286	
Accumulated Depreciation		$14,286

4. On April 1ˢᵗ, of the current year, the company purchased a 24 month insurance policy and paid $72,000. The payment was recorded to prepaid insurance.

	Prepaid Insurance	**Insurance Expense**
a) Which account names change?		
b) What type of account is changing?	Asset	Expense
c) Is the change to each account an increase or a decrease?	Decrease	Increase
d) Is the change to each account a debit or credit?	Credit	Debit

What should the balance be on December 31st?

Cost of $72,000 / 24 months = $3,000 per month
April 1ˢᵗ to December 31ˢᵗ is nine months used up.
Using up an asset is an expense: 9 months x $3,000 = $27,000 is the expense.

Cost per month	$ 3,000	
x Number of months passed	9	
= Adjustment to be made	$27,000	used up = expense

Make the adjusting entry to record the asset used up.

Insurance Expense	$27,000	
Prepaid Insurance		$27,000

5. On June 1ˢᵗ the company loaned $60,000 to another company in need of cash. The other company agreed to repay the full amount in two years and pay interest of eight percent annually each May 31st. Record the adjustment for the company that loaned the money.

	Interest Receivable	**Interest Revenue**
a) Which account names change?		
b) What type of account is changing?	Asset	Revenue
c) Is the change to each account an increase or a decrease?	Increase	Increase
d) Is the change to each account a debit or credit?	Debit	Credit

What should the balance be as of December 31st?

Interest = principle x rate x time: $60,000 x .08 x 7/12 months = $2,800
June 1 to December 31ˢᵗ is seven months earned this year.

Make the adjusting entry to record the revenue earned as time passed.

Interest Receivable	$2,800	
Interest Revenue		$2,800

6. On March 1ˢᵗ, the company borrowed $250,000 from the bank to be repaid in three years. The bank charges interest at an annual rate of 6 percent. Interest must be paid each year on February 28ᵗʰ.

a) Which account names change?	**Interest Expense**	**Interest Payable**
b) What type of account is changing?	Expense	Liability
c) Is the change to each account an increase or a decrease?	Increase	Increase
d) Is the change to each account a debit or credit?	Debit	Credit

What should the balance be as of December 31st?

Interest = principle x rate x time: $250,000 x .06 x 10 /12 months = $12,500

March 1ˢᵗ to December 31ˢᵗ is ten months incurred this year.

Make the adjusting entry to record the expense incurred as time passed.

Interest Expense	$12,500	
Interest Payable		$12,500

7. On August 1ˢᵗ the company received cash from a customer in the amount of $7,200 for services to be provided equally over the next six months. The service was provided monthly beginning on August 1ˢᵗ. The receipt of cash was recorded as unearned revenue.

a) Which account names change?	**Unearned Revenue**	**Service Revenue**
b) What type of account is changing?	Liability	Revenue
c) Is the change to each account an increase or a decrease?	Decrease	Increase
d) Is the change to each account a debit or credit?	Debit	Credit

What should the balance be as of December 31st?

$7,200 / 6 month = $1,200 per month

August 1ˢᵗ to December 31ˢᵗ is five months earned.
5 months x $1,200 per month = $6,000 earned

Make the adjusting entry to record the revenue earned.

Unearned Revenue	$6,000	
Service Revenue		$6,000

8. During the month of December the company provided services to a customer totaling $7,000. The accounting department did not know about the service and did not send an invoice.

	Accounts Receivable	Service Revenue
a) Which account names change?	**Accounts Receivable**	**Service Revenue**
b) What type of account is changing?	Asset	Revenue
c) Is the change to each account an increase or a decrease?	Increase	Increase
d) Is the change to each account a debit or credit?	Debit	Credit

What should be recorded?   Services in the amount of $7,000 were provided.
The customer owes $7,000.

Make the adjusting entry to record the revenue earned.

Accounts Receivable $7,000
    Service Revenue $7,000

The adjusting entry records the amount earned or incurred from the date of the original transaction or the date of the last adjusting entry to the end of the current period. The amount is computed as follows:

Revenue or expense per month:
$$\frac{\text{Total Dollars Paid}}{\text{Number of Months during the period}}$$

Interest expense or
interest revenue:

Principle owed
x Annual interest rate percent
x Number of Months in the current period / 12
= Interest expense or interest revenue

Annual Depreciation expense:
$$\frac{\text{Cost } - \text{ Residual Value}}{\text{The Useful Life of the Asset in years}}$$

The annual depreciation expense x # months / 12 = expense for the period

General rules related to adjusting entries follow:

1) When expenses increase, an asset decreases or a liability increases.

2) When revenue increases, an asset increases or unearned revenue decreases.

3) The cash account is not used in adjusting entries (with the exception of the bank reconciliation adjusting entry not discussed in this book.)

4) Revenues and expenses are reduced only when a revenue or expense was recorded at an amount greater than was earned or incurred. This occurs when an estimate was different from what actually occurred or the accounts payable clerk recorded an amount to the wrong account.

Adjusting entries are recorded to the same T account as original entries to get adjusted final balances that are reported on the financial statements.

Accountants identify adjustments that need to be made by looking at a list of all accounts and balances before adjustments are made. This list of accounts is called an **unadjusted trial balance** or an unadjusted general ledger.

Example A3-2 provides some insight into the thoughts of an accountant looking at a list of accounts when making adjustments. The list of accounts, also called the unadjusted trial balance, of the company reported the following:

Accounts	Debit	Credit
Cash	37,750	
Accounts Receivable	62,000	
Inventory	13,000	
Office Supplies	250	
Prepaid Insurance	7,200	
Short-term Investments	45,000	
Notes Receivable	5,000	
Equipment	41,000	
Trademarks	1,300	
Accounts Payable		0
Unearned Revenue		2,000
Short-term Notes Payable		32,000
Common Stock		150,000
Sales		62,000
Cost of Goods Sold	32,000	
Wage Expense	1,500	
Total	246,000	246,000

Example A3-2 continued

Questions asked by the accountant to determine if an adjusting entry should be made are as follows:

1) Does the company expect all accounts receivable to be collected? If not, an adjustment must be made to report the estimated amount that is not expected to be received. This will reduce accounts receivable to the amount of the probable future economic benefit.

2) Does the company actually have inventory in the warehouse that cost $13,000? If not, an adjustment must be made to report the cost of inventory the company actually has at the end of the period.

3) Does the company actually have office supplies on hand that cost $250? If not, an adjustment must be made to report the amount of office supplies the company actually owns at the end of the period.

4) Has the benefit of insurance coverage expired as time passed? If so, prepaid insurance must be reduced for the cost of coverage provided (used up) during the period. Prepaid insurance must be reported at the amount of the future benefit.

5) Have earnings from short-term investments been recorded? If not, the revenue from interest or dividends and the receivable must be recorded.

6) Has the interest revenue associated with notes receivable been recorded? If not, interest revenue and interest receivable must be calculated and recorded.

7) Has the expense of using the equipment and trademarks during the period been recorded? If not, depreciation and amortization expense must be estimated and recorded.

8) Has the interest expense associated with the short-term notes payable been recorded? If not, the interest expense and interest payable must be calculated and recorded. Interest does not change the amount of principle owed.

9) Have all services that the accountant knows are received monthly been recorded (even if an invoice has not yet been received?) If not, record more expense and accounts payable.

10) Does the amount of unearned revenue equal the current value of goods or services owed to customers? Has the company provided goods or services to customers who paid in a previous period? An adjustment to increase revenue and reduce unearned revenue may be needed.

A-4 Finishing the Accounting and Reporting Process

Accountants refer to the process of preparing financial statements at the end of each month (or quarter or year) as "closing the books." Closing the books consists of the steps listed below. Many of the steps were discussed previously in the Appendix. This portion of the Appendix will focus on steps seven through twelve required to prepare the financial statements.

The steps to preparing financial statements are as follows:

1) Transactions affecting cash and sales to customers are recorded as part of routine accounting procedures and data entered into the accounting system.

2) Journal entry amounts are recorded and subtotaled in "T" accounts.

3) An **unadjusted trial balance** is prepared. This is a listing of all accounts and **preliminary balances** before adjustments. The purpose of the unadjusted trial balance is to help the accountant identify accounts that need to be adjusted. An unadjusted trial balance is formatted as follows:

Account Name	Debit	Credit
Cash	50,000	
Accounts Receivable	30,000	
Inventory	20,000	
Equipment	78,000	
Accumulated Depreciation		15,000
Accounts Payable		10,000
Long-term Notes Payable		100,000
Common Stock		5,000
Retained Earnings (beginning)		43,000
Revenues		65,000
Expenses	60,000	
	238,000	238,000

A trial balance is also referred to as the "general ledger."

4) **Adjusting entries** are made to record transactions with no physical exchange that were not recorded automatically recorded through daily processes and accounting procedures.

5) Amounts in adjusting journal entries are recorded in each "T" account and a **final balance** for each account is determined.

6) An **adjusted trial balance** is prepared. All accounts and **final balances** are listed in the same format as the unadjusted trial balance.

7) An **income statement** is prepared. All revenue, expense, gain, and loss accounts and associated amounts on the adjusted trial balance are reported on the income statement. See chapter 5 for further discussion.

8) **Prepare closing entries**. Closing entries transfer all income statement accounts (revenues, expenses, gains, and losses) and dividends to the retained earnings account. Income statement accounts are called **temporary (or nominal) accounts** because they must start at zero at the beginning of each period in order for amounts to represent the current period only.
Accounts that change retained earnings are closed (made equal to zero) using the following three steps:

1) **Adjust all expense and loss accounts** to zero and transfer the amounts to retained earnings.

Retained earnings	*$XXXXX*	
_____*expense*		*$XXX*
_____ *expense*		*$XXX*
_____ *expense*		*$XXX*
_____ *expense*		*$XXX*
Cost of goods sold		*$XXX*
Loss on sale		*$XXX*

All expense and loss accounts have a debit balance. A credit to the account for the total amount changes the account balance to zero. Retained earnings is debited for the total of all credit amounts.

2) **Adjust all revenue and gain accounts** to zero and transfer the amounts to retained earnings.

Sales	*$XXX*	
Interest income	*$ XX*	
Dividend income	*$ XX*	
Service revenue	*$XXX*	
Gain on sale	*$ XX*	
Retained earnings		*$XXXX*

All revenue and gain accounts have a credit balance. A debit to the account for the total amount changes the account balance to zero. Retained earnings is credited for the total of all debit amounts.

3) **Adjust the dividend account** to zero and transfer the amount to retained earnings. A credit for the total amount of dividends changes the dividend account balance to zero.

Retained earnings	*$XXX*	
Dividend		*$XXX*

Closing entries transfer all items on the income statement and dividends to the retained earning account. The final ending balance of retained earnings is reported on the balance sheet.

	Retained Earnings	
	Beginning Balance
Expenses	Revenues
Losses	Gains
Dividends	
	Ending Balance

Retained Earnings consists of cumulative profits and losses kept in the company since the first day of operations. Earnings and dividends for the current period must be included in retained earnings.

Balance sheet accounts are called permanent or real accounts.

Balance sheet accounts are not transferred to retained earnings and do not start over at the beginning of each period. Balance sheet accounts are cumulative from the first day the business began operations.

Assets and liabilities do not go away when a new period starts. These accounts begin each period with the prior period ending balance. Cumulative amounts change as transactions occur during the period.

9) The **statement of stockholders' equity** is prepared. Account names are listed across the top and a description of each transaction that occurred during the period that changed on owners' equity account is stated on the left side. Amounts are stated in the column of the accounts that change. The ending balances for all accounts on the statement of stockholders' equity are also reported on the balance sheet. See chapter 7 for further discussion

10) A **balance sheet** is prepared. Account names and the amounts for all assets, liabilities, and stockholders' equity on the adjusted trial balance are reported on the balance sheet in proper format. The balance sheet reports retained earnings <u>at the end of the period,</u> which includes current period earnings and dividends. See chapter 2 for further discussion.

11) The **statement of cash flows** is prepared. (The steps to prepare the cash flow statement are beyond the scope of this book.)

12) The **footnotes** to the financial statements are prepared. See chapter 9 for further discussion.

The accounting department performs every step in the accounting process at the end of the period (month, quarter, and year) to prepare financial statements. Closing the books and preparing financial statements normally takes between three days and three weeks. The time required is dependent on the size of the company and the number of automated steps in the process.

Accountants must make sure the computer system recorded all automated transactions properly. Transactions that are not automatically recorded by the computer system through daily accounting procedures must be recorded as adjusting entries. Good controls must be in place to ensure all transactions are properly recorded. Incorrect or missing journal entries result in incorrect financial information.

Example A4-1 on the following pages illustrates each step in the closing process. Follow each step carefully all the way through to understand how recording transactions, adjusting entries, and closing entries provide the financial information necessary to prepare financial statements. Footnotes are not provided in this example.

Example A4-1: A Comprehensive Example of Preparing Financial Statements

A company had the following transactions during the month of January, <u>the first month of operations:</u>

1. Received $150,000 cash from investors for ownership in the company.
2. Purchased inventory at a cost of $45,000; on account.
3. Paid $7,200 for liability insurance for the entire year on January 2nd.
4. Sold inventory with a cost of $32,000 to customers for $62,000, on account.
5. Purchased manufacturing equipment that cost $39,000 (7 year life). Paid $7,000 cash and agreed to pay the balance plus interest in 6 months, 8% annual interest.
6. Employees worked and were paid $1,500 for the month.
7. Paid for the inventory purchased in (2.) above
8. Purchased office supplies for $250. ($100 remained at the end of January)
9. Paid for a trademark for the company at a cost of $1,300, 10 year life, not yet used.
10. Invested $50,000 in a short-term certificate of deposit earning a 6% annual rate. Interest will be collected February 1st next year.

The steps to preparing financial statements for the **month of January** are as follows:

Record the Initial Transaction

1. Received $150,000 cash from investors for ownership in the company.

    Received – Cash
    Gave up – Ownership

    Cash is an asset, increasing: debit
    Common Stock is stockholders' equity, increasing: credit

Cash	**$150,000**
Common stock	**$150,000**

2. Purchased inventory at a cost of $45,000; on account.

    Received – Inventory
    Gave up – A liability, accounts payable: "On account" means pay later

    Inventory is an asset, increasing: debit
    Accounts payable is a liability, increasing: credit

Inventory	**$45,000**
Accounts Payable	**$45,000**

3. *Paid $7,200 for liability insurance for the entire year on January 2nd.*

        Received – Insurance coverage in the future; Prepaid Insurance
        Gave up – Cash

        Prepaid insurance is an asset, increasing: debit
        Cash is an asset, decreasing: credit

Prepaid Insurance	**$7,200**	
Cash		**$7,200**

4. *Sold inventory with a cost of $32,000 to customers for $62,000, on account.*

        Received – Accounts receivable is an asset, increased: debit
        Provided Goods – Sales Revenue, increased: credit

        Gave up – Provided goods to customer, inventory decreases: credit
        Used an asset inventory, expense called cost of goods sold: debit

Accounts Receivable	**$62,000**	
Sales Revenue		**$62,000**
Cost of Goods Sold	**$32,000**	
Inventory		**$32,000**

5. *Purchased manufacturing equipment that cost $39,000 (7 year life). Paid $7,000 cash and agreed to pay the balance plus interest in 6 months, 8% annual interest.*

        Received – Equipment $39,000
        Gave up – Cash $7,000
        Gave up – Pay later, short-term notes payable

        Equipment is an asset, increasing: debit
        Cash is an asset, decreasing: credit
        Short-term notes payable is a liability, increasing: credit

Equipment	**$39,000**	
Cash		**$ 7,000**
S/T Notes Payable		**$32,000**

6. *Employees worked and were paid $1,500 for the month.*

    Received – A service, employees worked: wage expense
    Gave up – Cash

    Wages expense is an expense, increasing: debit
    Cash is an asset, decreasing: credit

Wages Expense	$1,500	
Cash		$1,500

7. *Paid for the inventory purchased in 2 above.*

    Received – Owe less, decreases accounts payable
    Gave up – Cash

    Accounts payable is a liability, decreasing: debit
    Cash is an asset, decreasing: credit

Accounts Payable	$45,000	
Cash		$45,000

8. *Purchased office supplies for $250 ($100 remained at the end of January.)*

    Received – Office Supplies
    Gave up – Cash

    Office supplies is an asset, increasing: debit
    Cash is an asset, decreasing: credit

Office Supplies	$250	
Cash		$250

9. *Paid for a trademark for the company at a cost of $1,300, 10 year life, not yet used.*

    Received – Trademark
    Gave up – Cash

    Trademark is an asset, increasing: debit
    Cash is an asset, decreasing: credit

Trademark	$1,300	
Cash		$1,300

10. *Invested $50,000 in a short-term certificate of deposit earning a 6% annual rate.*
    Interest will be collected February 1ˢᵗ next year.

       Received – Short-term Investment
       Gave up - Cash

       S/T Investment is an asset, increasing: debit
       Cash is an asset, decreasing: credit

Short-term Investment	**$50,000**
Cash	**$50,000**

T Accounts for Journal Entries: Steps 2, 4, and 5

Make a "T" account for each account, record all journal entry amounts in the T accounts on the proper debit or credit side, and balance each account. Adjusting entries made in step 4 are indicated with an "A" out to the side of the amount.

	Cash				Common Stock				Inventory	
(1)	150,000	7,200	(2)			150,000	(1)	(2)	45,000	32,000	(
		7,000	(5)							
		1,500	(6)							13,000
		45,000	(7)			**150,000**				
		250	(8)							
		1,300	(9)							
		50,000	(10)							
	150,000	112,250								
	37,750									

	Accounts Payable		
(7)	45,000	45,000	(2)
		0	

	Prepaid Insurance		
(3)	7,200		
		600	A
	6,600		

	Accounts Receivable		
(4)	62,000		
	62,000		

	Sales		
		62,000	(4)
		62,000	

	Cost of Goods Sold		
(4)	32,000		
	32,000		

	Equipment		
(5)	39,000		
	39,000		

	Short-term Notes Payable		
		32,000	(5)
		32,000	

	Wage Expense		
(6)	1,500		
	1,500		

	Office Supplies		
(8)	250		
		150	A
	100		

	Trademark		
(9)	1,300		
	1,300		

	Short-term Investments		
(10)	50,000		
	50,000		

	Insurance Expense		
A	600		
	600		

	Depreciation Expense
A	464
464	

	Accumulated Depreciation
	464 A
	464

	Interest Expense
A	213
213	

	Interest Payable
	213 A
	213

	Office Supplies Expense
A	150
150	

	Interest Receivable
A	250
250	

	Interest Revenue
	250 A
	250

	Retained Earnings
	0
	Beginning
	62,250 C
C 34,927	
	27,323

"C" is for closing entries

Step 3) Prepare an Unadjusted Trial Balance before Adjusting Journal Entries

Unadjusted Trial Balance

Accounts	Debit	Credit
Cash	37,750	
Accounts Receivable	62,000	
Inventory	13,000	
Office Supplies	250	
Prepaid Insurance	7,200	
Short-term Investments	50,000	
Equipment	39,000	
Trademarks	1,300	
Accounts Payable		0
Short-term Notes Payable		32,000
Common Stock		150,000
Sales		62,000
Cost of Goods Sold	32,000	
Wage Expense	1,500	
Total	244,000	244,000

Step 4) Prepare Adjusting Journal Entries for the Month of January
The transaction number on the right refers to the original transaction related to the adjustment.

Assets used during the month of January are recorded as follows:

3. Insurance Expense	600		$7,200 / 12 months = $600 each month
Prepaid Insurance		600	

5. Depreciation Expense	464		$39,000 / 7 years = $5,571 each year
Accumulated Depreciation		464	$5,571 / 12 months = $464 each month

8. Office Supplies Expense	150		$250 purchased - $100 ending = $150 used
Office Supplies		150	

9. No expense because the trademark was not used in January.

One month of a service provided (5. to the company and 10. to another entity) during January is recorded as follows:

5. Interest Expense	213		$32,000 x 8% x 1/12 = $213 each month
Interest Payable		213	

10. Interest Receivable	250		$50,000 x 6% x 1/12 = $250 each month
Interest Revenue		250	

Step 5) Record the Adjusting Journal Entry Amounts in the T Accounts and Balance the T accounts

See the previous T accounts. Adjustments are noted with an "A" beside the amounts.

Step 6) Prepare an Adjusted Trial Balance with FINAL Accounts and Amounts

List every account name with a T account and the final balance in the T account in the correct column.

Accounts	Debit	Credit
Cash	37,750	
Accounts Receivable	62,000	
Inventory	13,000	
Office Supplies	100	
Prepaid Insurance	6,600	
Interest Receivable	250	
Short-term Investments	50,000	
Equipment	39,000	
Accumulated Depreciation		464
Trademarks	1,300	
Accounts Payable		0
Interest Payable		213
Short-term Notes Payable		32,000
Common Stock		150,000
Sales		62,000
Cost of Goods Sold	32,000	
Wage Expense	1,500	
Insurance Expense	600	
Depreciation Expense	464	
Office Supplies Expense	150	
Interest Expense	213	
Interest Revenue		250
Total	244,927	244,927

Step 7) Prepare an Income Statement for the Month of January.

All revenues and expenses listed on the adjusted trial balance are reported on the income statement.

Sales	62,000	
- Cost of Goods Sold	32,000	
= Gross Profit	30,000	
- Operating Expenses:		
Wage Expense	1,500	
Insurance Expense	600	
Depreciation Expense	464	
Office Supplies Expense	150	
= Income from Operations	27,286	
Interest Expense	(213)	
Interest Revenue	250	This example has no
= Net Income	27,323	income tax expense.

Step 8) Prepare Closing Journal Entries

All revenue, expense, gain, loss, and dividend accounts are transferred to retained earnings.

Sales	62,000	
Interest Revenue	250	
Gain on Sale of Assets	0	
Retained Earnings		62,250 (total of all debits)

Retained Earnings	34,927 (total of all credits)	
Cost of Goods Sold		32,000
Wage Expense		1,500
Insurance Expense		600
Depreciation Expense		464
Office Supplies Expense		150
Interest Expense		213
Loss on Sale of Assets		0

There were no dividends in this example. The closing entry for dividends is:

Retained Earnings	0	
Dividends		0

Step 9) Prepare a Statement of Stockholders' Equity for the Month of January

	Common Stock	Retained Earnings
January 1, 20XX	$ 0	$ 0
Issued Common Stock	$150,000	$ 0
Net Income		$27,323
January 31, 20XX	$150,000	$27,323

The final ending amounts on the statement of stockholders' equity are reported on the balance sheet.

Step 10) Prepare a Balance Sheet as of January 31st

List all assets, liabilities and stockholders' equity accounts and the final balances on the adjusted trial balance in proper format.

Assets		Liabilities	
Cash	37,750	Interest Payable	213
Accounts Receivable	62,000	Short-term Notes Payable	32,000
Inventory	13,000		
Office Supplies	100		
Prepaid Insurance	6,600	Total Current Liabilities	32,213
Interest Receivable	250		
Short-term Investment	50,000		
Total Current Assets	169,700	Total Liabilities	32,213
		Owner's Equity	
P/P/E:			
Equipment	39,000	Common Stock	150,000
- Accumulated Depreciation	(464)	Retained Earnings	27,323
Net P/P/E:	38,536	Total Owner's Equity	177,323
Intangible Assets:			
Trademark	1,300		
		Total Liabilities and	
Total Assets	209,536	Owner's Equity	209,536

Step 11) Prepare a Statement of Cash Flows using the Direct Method

Cash collected from customers	$ 0
Cash paid for supplies	(250)
Cash paid for inventory	(45,000)
Cash paid to employees	(1,500)
Cash paid for insurance	(7,200)
Cash used for operating activities	(53,950)
Equipment purchased	(7,000)
Trademark purchased	(1,300)
Short-term investments purchased	(50,000)
Cash used for investing activities	(58,300)
Common stock issued	150,000
Cash from financing activities	150,000
Total Change in Cash	$ 37,750
Beginning Cash	0
Ending Cash	$ 37,750

Company Reference

Annual 10-K as of:	Company	Pages
September 23, 2011	Apple, Inc.	114-125
February 26, 2011	Best Buy, Inc.	27
December 31, 2010	Chipotle Mexican Grill, Inc.	60, 84
December 31, 2011	FaceBook, Inc.	144-146
December 31, 2011	General Electric	61
December 31, 2011	Google, Inc.	114-125
January 28, 2012	Home Depot, Inc.	114-125
December 25, 2010	Intel Corporation	58, 111-112
February 2, 2012	The Lowes Companies	114-125
June 30, 2011	Microsoft, Inc.	73-74
June 30, 2010	PepsiCo. Inc.	29
June 30, 2011	PepsiCo. Inc.	141-142
January 28, 2012	Sears Holding Company	138-140
January 30, 2010	Target Corporation	97
October 1, 2011	Walt Disney Company	3-8, 86, 99-105

Index of Topics

	Page
Accounting Equation	32, 147
Accounts	31, 147
Accounts Payable	14, 66
Accounts Receivable	66
Accounts Receivable Turnover	119
Accrual Basis of Accounting	45
Accrued Expenses	67
Accrued Liabilities	67
Accumulated Amortization	53
Accumulated Depreciation	51, 52
Adjusted Trial Balance	177
Adjusting Journal Entries	169
Amortization Expense	53
Annual Report	107
Assets	11, 17
Auditor's Report	10, 12
Bad Debt Expense	70
Bonds Payable	15
Cash	17
Cash Basis of Accounting	45
Cash Equivalents	18
Cash Flow Adequacy	96
Closing Entries	178
Commercial Paper	14
Common Size Analysis	110
Common Stock	13, 22
Cost of Goods Sold	50, 70
Credit	155
Current Ratio	116
Days to Collect	119
Debit	155
Deferred Revenue	65
Depreciation Expense	51
Direct Method of the Cash Flow Statement	91
Dividends	22
Double Entry Bookkeeping	155
Earned	39

Index of Topics

	Page
Earnings per Share	62, 124
Estimates Used by Accountants	127
Expense	39, 49, 70
Fair Market Value of a Total Company	136
Financial Accounting Standards Board	9
Financing Activities	87
Financing Receivables	19
Footnotes	99
Free Cash Flow	95
Gains	40
Generally Accepted Accounting Standards	9
Gift Cards	71
Goodwill	20, 133
Gross Profit Margin	55, 121
Historical Cost	26
Income Tax Expense	57, 133
Incurred	39
Indirect Method of the Cash Flow Statement	88
Intangible Assets	20, 53, 131
International Accounting Standards Board	10
International Financial Reporting Standards	10
Inventory	18, 50, 128
Inventory Turnover	118
Investing Activities	87
Investments	18
Journal Entry	155
Liabilities	14
Liquidity	24
Long-term Debt	15
Loss Contingencies	132
Losses	40
Marketable Securities	18
Multi-step Income Statement	55
Notes Payable	15
Notes Receivable	19
Operating Activities	87
Operating Profit Margin	121

Index of Topics

	Page
Other Comprehensive Income	24
Preferred Stock	22
Prepaid Expense	19, 51, 66
Price to Earnings	124
Profit Margin	122
Property, Plant, and Equipment	19, 51, 131
Public Company Accounting Oversight Board	10
Quick Ratio	116
Ratio Analysis	114
Retained Earnings	23, 152
Return on Assets	122
Return on Equity	123
Revenue	39, 49, 65
Securities Exchange Commission	10
Securities Exchange Commission Reports	106
Single Step Income Statement	59
Stock and Capital	13, 21
Stockholders' Equity	11, 21, 83
Straight-line Method of Depreciation	51
Supplies	18, 50, 70
T Accounts	156
Temporary Accounts	178
Transaction	31
Treasury Stock	23
Unadjusted Trial Balance	177
Unearned Revenue	65
Warranties	131